GROWING IN LOVE WITH Catherine of Siena

GROWING IN LOVE WITH
Catherine of Siena

Diana L. Villegas

Paulist Press
New York / Mahwah, NJ

Illustrations by Paula A. Gomez

Scripture quotations are from the New Revised Standard Version Bible: Catholic Edition, copyright © 1989, 1993 National Council of the Churches of Christ in the United States of America. Used by permission. All rights reserved worldwide.

Cover image by Paula A. Gomez
Cover and book design by Lynn Else

Library of Congress Cataloging-in-Publication Data
Names: Villegas, Diana author
Title: Growing in love with Catherine of Siena / Diana L. Villegas;illustrations by Paula A. Gomez.
Description: New York: Paulist Press, [2025] | Includes bibliographical references. | Summary: "This book is a selection of passages of Catherine of Siena's wisdom presented with meditations and prayer exercises"—Provided by publisher.
Identifiers: LCCN 2024051580 (print) | LCCN 2024051581 (ebook) | ISBN 9780809157594 paperback | ISBN 9780809189267 ebook
Subjects: LCSH: Catherine, of Siena, Saint, 1347–1380—Meditations | Spiritual life—Catholic Church
Classification: LCC BX4700.C4 V55 2025 (print) | LCC BX4700.C4 (ebook) | DDC 282.092—dc23/eng/20250527
LC record available at https://lccn.loc.gov/2024051580
LC ebook record available at https://lccn.loc.gov/2024051581

ISBN 978-0-8091-5759-4 (paperback)
ISBN 978-0-8091-8926-7 (ebook)

Published by Paulist Press
997 Macarthur Boulevard
Mahwah, NJ 07430
www.paulistpress.com

Printed and bound in the
United States of America

Contents

Acknowledgements vii

Introduction 1

1. Created out of Love for Love 19

   Pictorial Meditation 1: Birthed from God 25

2. Recognizing God's Loving Presence 27

3. The Inner Cell 32

4. Two Cells in One 37

5. The Cell as Well: *I-Am-Not*—God IS 43

6. The Cell: Going to Bed 49

7. We Are a Tree of Love 54

8. Fruit of a Well-Planted Tree 61

   Pictorial Meditation 2: Well-Planted Tree 69

9. Free Will and Love 71

10. Angelic Food 78

CONTENTS

11. Angelic Food and Transformation 83

12. Memory, Understanding, and Will 90

13. The Eye of Understanding 98

14. The Blood of Christ 105

15. Christ's Blood and Knowledge of Self 111

16. Christ's Blood as Mortar 116

Pictorial Meditation 3: The Blood of Christ—
Life-Giving Water 123

17. Stairs Up the Body of Christ 125

18. Pray to Mother Mary 132

Notes 137

For Further Reading 139

Acknowledgements

I AM VERY GRATEFUL to Paula A. Gomez, talented design artist, who, despite her busy schedule as artistic director in a publicity firm, took time to create the images for the pictorial meditations. Her exceptional work enriches this book in a significant manner.

I thank Phil Daughtry, PhD, spiritual director and scholar of spirituality, for reviewing this manuscript and offering most valuable feedback.

Introduction

WOULD YOU LIKE TO GROW in capacity to love aided by the wisdom of Catherine of Siena? This book would like to assist you on such a journey. For Catherine's spirituality is focused on the scriptural truth that we are created in the image of God with capacity to love because God is love. All of her wisdom and advice comes back to this central belief. The spiritual journey involves developing a relationship with God so that we can cooperate with God's transforming love and become the persons we are meant to be. In this way we fulfill our calling as children of God—which brings peace and joy—and we are able to act in life in a way that contributes to God's desires and values as we engage in our personal life and in relating to our community.

The journey offered here invites the reader-seeker on a path along eighteen reflections and three pictorial meditations. Each reflection offers extracts from Catherine's letters with explanations about her wisdom, scripture passages with related biblical wisdom, and a set of proposed spiritual exercises aimed at living out Catherine's teachings. The pictorial meditations offer symbolic representations of Catherine's metaphorical wisdom with suggestions for engaging in contemplation of these images.

In this introduction you will find a summary of Catherine's life, a brief reflection about her reputation as a great mystic, and a summary of her spiritual doctrine.[1] The second part of this introduction features guidelines for the practice of the proposed spiritual exercises.

Catherine's Life[2]

Catherine lived from 1347 to 1380 in Siena in the Italian region of Tuscany. She was the twenty-fourth child of her parents, one of a set of twins; the other twin died shortly after birth. Her father was in the wool dyeing business and considered a prosperous merchant, so she was part of a large extended family who lived together in a home that was also the seat of the business. Catherine grew up learning how to be a woman who would one day be a matron of such an extended family. This did not include any kind of schooling or any education in how to read or write.

Religious formation occurred through the family and through often daily participation in parish devotions, especially the celebration of the Liturgy of the Hours (Divine Office) and the Mass. During these services, the Dominican friars of Catherine's local church preached in order to form the mostly illiterate parishioners. Also contributing to Catherine's early religious formation was one of her cousins—brought up in her home—who became a Dominican friar and for a time worked out of the nearby Dominican church.

At age six Catherine had a vision of Christ that led her to a deep sense of the reality of God and instilled in her a profound desire to give herself to God. She clearly experienced a deeply felt sense of God's love for her that led to her lifelong desire for a close relationship with God. When she was around fifteen years of age, when girls in Siena were promised in marriage, she cut off her hair, a rebellious and symbolic act that told her family she was serious about not marrying, for she had already promised herself exclusively to Jesus. She intended to devote herself to a life of intercessory prayer, something she had already been practicing at home since her childhood. Eventually her parents relented, first her father and then her mother, and allowed her to join the Siena *Mantellate*.

While most people think of Catherine as a nun, she was not. She was a member of the Siena *Mantellate,* a medieval penitent order similar to but not fully like a lay third order today within the Catholic tradition. In the Middle Ages these orders of penitents consisted of groups of women who were widowed or not married, who lived at home and wanted to devote themselves to a deepened life of prayer. The women made no vows and were not officially affiliated to a religious order but were offered guidance by priests of different orders; the Siena *Mantellate* were guided by the Dominicans, who offered Catherine and her fellow penitents regular spiritual guidance.

In this medieval context, some lay persons who committed themselves to a life of prayer often acquired reputations for holiness and wisdom; they were then sought out by fellow town persons for intercessory prayer and wise advice. Catherine became such a person in Siena, sought after by members of Siena's ruling classes as well as by others. She became known for the conversion of many young men as well as for helping settle disputes among men and among whole families. During the plague, which decimated a large part of Siena's population, Catherine became active in nursing victims and prayed successfully for the healing of some.

Having become known for holiness and wisdom, when she was twenty-seven, she was taken under the wing of the Dominican friars by order of high church authorities, with the goal of guiding her flowering gifts and directing her ministry toward the needs of the church. As her spiritual director she was assigned Friar Raymond of Capua, a learned friar and leader in the order. He instructed her in theology and church politics, guiding her ministry to a church in great need of reform and involved in tumultuous political struggles. Through Raymond's guidance Catherine's ministry shifted to a mission beyond Siena during the last six years of her short life.

In the mid-fourteenth century, the church was embroiled in political conflicts, and, most concerning to Catherine, the pastoral leaders of the church were often more involved with their status as lords of lands than their roles as pastors. Italy as a country did not exist. Instead, there were regions that were under the rule of European monarchies, a series of independent city-states in Tuscany, and a large section in the middle of today's Italy that belonged to the Papal States, whose temporal head was the pope. Since 1309 these States were governed by representatives of popes who themselves lived in Avignon, France. There were repeated conflicts between the Papal States and the Tuscan Republics, namely, Florence, Siena, Pisa, and Lucca. Under the guidance of Friar Raymond, Catherine became deeply involved in advocacy for the cause of the Papal States, which was most often related to power and control of territory rather than to issues of faith. Catherine was concerned that brothers were fighting brothers, that there was no peace and therefore no space for the church to focus on reforming itself and devoting itself more to pastoral care. She also advocated for a crusade, which she rather naively imagined would enable peace in Europe and increase conversions; the crusade never took place in Catherine's time. Catherine strongly lobbied Pope Gregory XI to return to Rome from Avignon; for she became convinced that for the church to move toward reform and give priority to pastoral care, it was essential for the pope to reside in Rome.[3] After the death of Gregory XI, during the last two years of her life, Catherine advocated for the legitimacy of Urban VI, who followed Gregory, but whose papacy was contested by an alternative pope elected in 1378 and installed in Avignon.

During the time of her public ministry Catherine continued to offer pastoral care to those brought to her attention, and she engaged in extensive correspondence, as will be described below. Also, she continued to devote herself to lengthy periods of prayer, focusing on intercession for those close to her, for those brought to her attention, but most of all for all the causes concerning the church she loved. Her ascetical practices, fasting and penance, were all experienced as forms of intercessory prayer. The disordered lives of clergy and even of the pope caused her deep sorrow. She offered these sufferings and her severe physical and at times spiritual afflictions for the reform of the church and for the transformation of the pope and clergy.

Catherine moved to Rome during the last year and a half of her life and died there at age thirty-three.

Catherine's Writings

Catherine left us her spiritual wisdom in a book titled *The Dialogue*, in 383 letters, and in twenty-six prayers. (See "For Further Reading" for English editions of these works.) Catherine dictated these works to her followers who knew how to read and write, as she only learned to read probably after age twenty-five and perhaps acquired the rudiments of writing in the last two and a half years of her life. *The Dialogue* is written primarily in the voice of God responding to Catherine regarding petitions for the reform of the church, for the world, for her spiritual guide Raymond of Capua, and for an anonymous sinner. There have been many scholarly debates regarding the extent to which Catherine dictated words she heard in ecstasy. Undoubtedly, some of *The Dialogue* reflects this spiritual experience, but not all, and there is evidence that Catherine eventually edited parts of the text.

The Dialogue is divided into several sections with very short chapters. The first several sections include the core of Catherine's wisdom about the spiritual journey, her wisdom about who persons are from God's perspective, what God expects of us, and how we grow toward those expectations. There is a section on God's providence, one on the church and the priesthood, and a concluding section about obedience, starting with Christ's obedience to God. In reading the profound wisdom Catherine expresses in *The Dialogue*, we must keep in mind that all visions and words—even those of the greatest mystics—reflect God's power acting in a particular human person, living at a particular moment in history and in a particular culture. Accordingly, the images, the language, and the formulations of mystical experience will have an essence of God's truth but will have much that is culturally and historically conditioned. Thus, God's words to Catherine in *The Dialogue* must be read through this lens and not considered absolute.

The Letters

One of Catherine's most important ministries was her letter writing, which started in earnest in 1374, when she was twenty-seven. She penned missives to married persons, to widows, to young men, to doctors and lawyers and artists. She engaged in intense correspondence with church and temporal leaders, with knights and political leaders; and of course, with nuns, friars, monks, and priests and with the members of her penitent order. All these letters aimed primarily to encourage the recipients to transform their lives, to grow in knowledge of God's love and in commitment to a life that allowed for a relationship with God. For Catherine was convinced that a pope could not be a good leader, a knight could not be a good warrior, a housewife could not be a good mother and wife, a nun or friar could not be a good member of their religious order, unless they were engaged in a relationship with God that allowed for transformation by God's love.

While all of Catherine's letters focused on the foregoing goal, she also offered advice. In the case of her missives to political and church leaders, she suggested actions that would lead to peace and transformation of the church. In the case of Pope Gregory XI, she urged him not to delay carrying out a crusade and not to delay his move to Rome. When Urban VI was challenged by another cardinal that was also elected pope, Catherine wrote a number of letters urging fidelity to Urban VI.

Catherine had a literary gift. She expressed herself in her own distinctive manner, using language in a way that was unique even for the fourteenth-century Siena in which she lived; and she used metaphors worthy of a poet. Her wisdom about how to live life according to God's law of love is shared with passionate language, with powerful images, and with practical common sense. But this powerful, creative communication can be difficult to fully understand because her creative metaphors and style are often not obvious to a twenty-first-century reader. The reflections in this volume seek to explain Catherine's language and metaphors, making her wisdom more user-friendly. Note that the translations reflect Catherine's dictated communication with its unique expressions; there is no attempt to make her communication elegant in English.[4]

Catherine as Saint and Mystic

Catherine's reputation as a woman mystic is based on the accounts of her hagiographers[5] about extraordinary visions from God and about her exceptional commitment to prayer, fasting, and penance. Medieval ideals of holiness favored heroic acts of penance, fasting, and self-denial, as well as exceptional visions, so these aspects were highlighted and even exaggerated and shaped to create a narrative of holiness. We know Catherine indeed experienced the reality of God's love, presence, and communication in extraordinary ways. However, in themselves her experiences of God are not what made her an extraordinary Christian. It was her response to God that made her exceptional; that is, her utter faithfulness in giving all of her life to follow God's will. Undoubtedly this response was made possible through the transforming power of God's love which she so unconditionally and wholeheartedly sought and received.

Catherine's letters are particularly revealing of her experience of God as transforming. The exhortations and advice to her correspondents reveal her intimacy with God and especially her utter faith and trust in God's love and action in her life giving her the inspiration and authority to speak to others in God's name. This faith and trust in God, and obedience to God's inner guidance to preach and exhort are most remarkable dimensions of her life. Though an uneducated young woman in a culture in which women had no authority unless they were abbesses or members of the high nobility, she acted and wrote with great authority, certain that God acted through her and that she was the bearer of God's wisdom and God's will for others. These others included church and political leaders and heads of monasteries. She expressed insight and advice with the certainty that God would intervene and help those she advised. We can only begin to imagine how filled Catherine was by the Spirit of God, when we consider how countercultural were her ministry and the authority she took on in all sorts of circles.

In her response to God, she herself lived the wisdom she left us about transformation in capacity to love and about caring for the good of the other as the main purpose and goal of our lives. Though she was certainly a mystic, Catherine was most exemplary in that she gave her life for the mission she felt God entrusted to her and did so with all her heart, all her energy, and all her creative gifts.

Doctrine about the Spiritual Journey

While Catherine is known for her mystical experience of God, her teaching, as we shall see, does not focus on how to pray or how to seek mystical experiences; rather, Catherine's wisdom is centered on how to pursue a journey of growth and transformation so that we become capable of the love for which we were created; we are intended to be fulfilled through the actualization and living out of that capacity. Accordingly, the spiritual journey entails the process of becoming changed into persons capable of loving as Jesus did so that we can contribute to God's world and the coming of God's kingdom. Bringing about God's kingdom starts with our closest family, with work relationships, and extends to all levels of our involvement in life. For becoming capable of love makes us persons who contribute to the ordered functioning of life around us and the blooming of God's values in our midst.

Love has many layers of meaning. Catherine refers to the gospel meaning of love, which entails the capacity to care for the good of the other, where the other is our family, our friends, our colleagues, our community, and today we would add our common home, the earth. Love involves the ability to take distance from our own needs and preferences and then to respond unselfishly according to the specific way in which each of us is called to be engaged in our family, our work, or a larger cause. Jesus embodied this love in that he devoted his public life to the mission entrusted him by God and pursued this mission with all his heart no matter the consequences. He left the comfort of his parents' home to become an itinerant preacher, teaching, healing, and offering God's mercy. This mission was a threat to many, so that he was persecuted and eventually killed. This willingness to do what is right, what one is called to do in one's particular life no matter what the cost, is the love to which we are called. This is the love Catherine preached and tried wholeheartedly to live herself. In this context, then, love does not refer to an emotion or to an attachment to someone, though the altruistic care for those to whom we are attached is part of Catherine's call to love.

Catherine's teaching about growth in knowledge of self and God implied learning the truth as an inherent part of God's law of love. In his preaching Jesus insisted on naming the truth about all sorts of topics important to the people of his time. For instance, he named who was a neighbor, challenging his fellow citizens to assist the marginalized; Jesus explained the truth about God's view of sinners and the need for compassion. Naming and seeing reality with truth has implications for our engagement in life for the good of the other and the common good. Truth similarly has to do with recognizing with honesty our own reality. Denial about our flaws, denial about the disorder of our life, denial about the injustices we accept in order to benefit ourselves, these are all forms of lack of truth. Catherine's wisdom urges the inner changes that make us capable of recognizing reality and that generate in us the desire to plead with God to help us live accordingly.

The Cell as Space for Knowledge of God and Self

How do we grow in this journey toward the capacity to love? Through knowledge of God and self. Knowledge of God involves felt experience and recognition of God's unfathomable love and endless mercy, a knowledge that impels a deep desire to receive that love, source of transformation. Knowledge of self is dual. One dimension is the other side of the coin of knowledge of God, that is, the recognition that we deeply need God's love. The other dimension is the journey of learning the truth about those aspects of our attitudes, beliefs, and actions that stem from a self-centered stance in life. For Catherine, the human tendency to view reality with ourselves at the center is the core of all disorder.

Catherine's repetitive exhortations about self-centeredness may seem harsh to the extent that they reflect a style of medieval piety that was not informed by our current psychological understanding about persons. Today we understand that our life story, especially in childhood and adolescence, has a strong influence on our capacity to give of ourselves. Thus, in receiving Catherine's teaching about selfish self-love, as she puts it, we keep in mind that this teaching is balanced by her absolute conviction and insistence on the unimaginable mercy and love God has for us. This means that in learning that we are loved by God, we learn compassion and mercy toward ourselves as we examine our self-centeredness. For some, the journey to a healthy self-love based on reception of God's love may be the first part of a spiritual path.

Given the foregoing formulation of the goals of the spiritual journey, Catherine repeatedly emphasized that we must spend time in the inner cell. The inner cell—sometimes cell of the soul, cell of self-knowledge, house of knowledge of self—is a metaphor for an inner space where our awareness and consciousness can sense and focus on God's presence. Thus, Catherine always exhorts her correspondents to spend time in this cell, that is, in silence and solitude, which are essential for a connection and felt relationship with God. (Chapters 3–6 impart Catherine's teaching on the cell and the dynamics of the spiritual journey.) For foundational to the spiritual journey is a relationship with God, and such a relationship requires the discipline to set aside the time and space required to pursue it.

Time in silence and solitude, centered on the presence of God, is also necessary to look at ourselves with truth, to recognize and own our weaknesses, vulnerabilities, and disordered points of view. It takes time to come to these realizations about ourselves and to allow space for God's grace to act; it takes time and space to sense and take in God's compassionate, healing love empowering change within us.

When we experience changes in ourselves after seeking help from God for emotional healing or help in overcoming wounded responses and behaviors, we experientially learn about God's care for our very particular needs; we experience God's transforming power for our specific reality. Such experience fuels our desire for greater connection to God. And as we seek further connection to God, we encounter further experiences of transformation. So for Catherine, knowledge of God is not primarily focused on having exceptional experiences. Rather, for Catherine knowledge of God is more focused on those times when we experience God's love, mercy, and compassion in response to our felt realization of our need for God. This dynamic dual knowledge allows us to grow in loving God, in depending on God, and in openness to receiving the grace that transforms us.

In the eighteen sections of this book, you will find Catherine's specific wisdom on the above themes, together with options for prayer experiences that will help you learn about Catherine's wisdom at a personally lived level.

Guide to Prayer Exercises

This book can be used in several ways, as spiritual reading and as information about Catherine's spiritual wisdom; or it can be used as an aid to prayer and meditation accompanied by Catherine's wisdom, or both. While there is an intended order to the chapters, the reflections and meditations could be done in any order that inspires the reader.

Each of the eighteen sections begins with excerpts from Catherine's letters related to her wisdom about transformation in capacity to love. Catherine repeats the core of this wisdom with many different metaphors, as her goal is to stir the hearts of her hearers to deeper understanding and motivation. Thus, though core insights are repeated, each chapter offers novel images that stir different dimensions of our imagination and emotional engagement and that point to fresh dimensions of the spiritual journey.

Scripture passages that present a biblical perspective on Catherine's teaching comprise the next section. These are followed by my interpretation of Catherine's excerpts in order to offer guidance in understanding her communication and the implications of her wisdom for a spiritual journey in today's culture.

Practical Recommendations

The practical suggestions at the end of each chapter include many approaches to prayer as different methods appeal to different persons. Also, different approaches to opening our consciousness to the presence of God will work for us at different moments of our life. No one method is *the* method for all or for every moment of life. Each reader is invited to pick those exercises to which they feel attracted rather than attempt to accomplish all those recommended.

Consciousness

Before describing the categories of prayer exercises offered with each reflection, I want to define the way I use a very important term, namely, *consciousness*. With this word I refer to awareness, particularly to the levels of awareness of inner experience. Normally our consciousness, our awareness, is tuned in to outer reality, to what is happening around us, to the tasks in which we are engaged, to interactions with others. At times, our attention is turned more inward, though still focused on a specific undertaking, as when we write or perform a task that requires deeper thought. When we want to pray, the goal is to turn our attention away from outer awareness and to our inner consciousness—inner focus and awareness—where we can more directly and consciously encounter the Spirit. As outer issues of daily life, or the many thoughts, images, preoccupations, and worries that float in our consciousness become more and more silent, then our awareness becomes more and more able to recognize the inner movements of the Spirit dwelling within us. When we focus on words of prayer, on an image, or on a set of words from scripture, part of the goal is to, as it were, change the topic in our consciousness to God and away from all that usually floats in our awareness. The goal of a breathing exercise, of a centering prayer exercise, of monastic lectio (to be explained below), is precisely to silence the more surface layers of awareness or consciousness. We encounter God present to us as our consciousness is increasingly open to inner spiritual reality, the presence of God within us.

Certainly, God's grace can touch us at any time, even when awareness is focused outwardly. We can suddenly feel God's love or presence, or suddenly sense an answer to a question we have been placing before God. Further, whenever we use our free will to choose to spend time in silence, even if our awareness is totally distracted and it seems that our consciousness remains busy with outer reality, God's love will be working in our heart and mind, because God always responds to a choice to spend time with God. We may not know how grace has touched us, but we can trust that it has. While keeping the foregoing in mind, a major goal of the prayer exercises offered in this book is to facilitate turning our consciousness inward in order to connect with the presence of God and God's communication with us.

Preparation for Prayer

Placing ourselves before God is an important start to a prayer period. Some may bless themselves, invoking the Trinity; some may informally say to God, here I am. Each person will address the person of the triune God with whom they are most comfortable. Is that Jesus, Holy Spirit, Spirit of God, Creator God, God my mother, or God my father? Sometimes we might invoke one person of the Trinity, while in another prayer period a different person is invoked. It is up to each of us to choose how to invoke God. The key is to address God in a way that emerges from our heart at the moment we are making our prayer.

Grace

After placing ourselves in God's presence, we ask for the recommended grace. The practice of asking for a particular grace during a prayer period serves several purposes. It focuses us on that which we need from God, on the spiritual growth we are seeking. Combined with the use of a prayer journal, it assists us in recognizing God's personal response and thus deepens and cements our relationship with God. Keeping a journal of graces requested and reflecting on how God has responded to these requests allows us to recognize God's very personal engagement with us, and such recognition then leads to growth in confidence that God hears us; this sort of reflection underlines in a felt way the very personal nature of God's care for us.

Centering Exercise

Our prayer periods are most fruitful if we start by quieting our mind as much as possible, for, as already mentioned, our minds are constantly busy with worries, plans, desires, and more. A centering exercise will help us let go of focusing on such "noise." Of course, we may want to concentrate our prayer period on a particular desire or worry, but we can do this after generally quieting our mind with a centering exercise. I recommend spending the first five to ten minutes of a prayer period focused on a centering exercise. Be aware that it is normal to be distracted during a centering exercise. Our mind will wander away from the chosen focus. At these times we simply "greet" the distraction and then return our attention to the chosen focus. Let go of thinking about what is going on; let go of any analysis of the experience. Let go and refocus on the focal point you have chosen.

I recommend several possible focal points:

1. Paying attention to our breathing so that our mind is focused on noticing when we breathe in and when we breathe out.
2. Adding words such as "Jesus" when I breathe in and "Lord" when I breathe out. Or "Come, Holy Spirit," or other invocations you may choose. This is equivalent to the method of the Jesus Prayer of Eastern monastics.
3. Focus on an object, such as a candle or an image of Christ or your favorite icon. As your mind wanders away from this focus, gently return your attention to the image or candle.
4. Play a set of tones or repetitive music meant to help quiet the mind and keep returning your awareness to the music.

Phrase for Monastic Lectio

I have coined this phrase to refer to the monastic practice of listening to a set of words from scripture while walking around the cloister or sitting in the refectory. The goal of this monastic exercise is to let a set of words touch our consciousness to see what thought, insight, or movement of the heart is stirred. We take time to repeat the words and let go of any effort of the mind to sort out their meaning or to work out what message they may convey. Rather, we let go interiorly and receive the words as rain falling on our consciousness, noticing as time passes and we keep repeating them—as the rain soaks in—which words become interiorly highlighted. This experience of words becoming highlighted occurs as a word or set of words attracts us, as a word or set of words seems to stick in our mind, as a set of words stirs an insight or something we want to say to God. Monastic lectio can be the centering exercise or a significant part of a prayer period or a whole prayer period.

Monastic lectio exercises in this book include words from scripture, Catherine's own words, or paraphrases of her words.

Imagination Prayer Exercises

These exercises are inspired by the images and metaphors Catherine offers. They suggest ways of using our imagination to facilitate the experience of God's communication with us. When we use our imagination, our consciousness is normally fully engaged, and the themes of our inner narrative become a vehicle for the Word of God to us. This type of prayer practice is often used with scripture, when we imagine a scene from a Gospel, for instance, in order to see how the scene comes alive and speaks to us.

1

Created out of Love for Love

Letter 16—Birthed of the Father

Catherine writes Jesus's words as she heard them in her heart:

> If the unimaginable love that I have for the human race had come to an end, if it had been exhausted, you would not exist. For through love you were birthed from the womb of my Father who created you with his wisdom, and so through love you are held together for you are made of nothing else but love. If he withheld this love filled with the power and wisdom with which he created you, you would cease to be.

Letter 86—Breast of Christ

My dearest mother, we should act like a child who, wanting milk, takes the breast of his mother, placing it in his mouth so that he takes in milk through her flesh.

We should act in this same way if we want to feed our soul. We should attach ourselves to the breast of Christ crucified, in whom is the mother of love, and through his flesh we take in the milk that feeds our soul and its children the virtues.

Scripture

Then God said, "Let us make humankind in our image, according to our likeness." So God created humankind in his image, in the image of God he created them. (Gen 2:26a, 27)

He chose us in Christ before the foundation of the world to be holy and blameless before him in love. (Eph 1:4)

Reflection

We are created out of love and for love! God, who is love, created us out of that love, a love that overflowed into creation. So out of the fullness of God's love, human persons came to exist. Catherine repeats this throughout her writings in images and metaphors. She states this in her words, in those of Jesus, and those of God the Father.

Think about the desire of couples to have a child; think about those couples who struggle through years of unpleasant and stressful fertility treatments. Think of the fortunes some spend trying to conceive a child. What drives and motivates these efforts to bear a child? At its best, it is the desire to create a human person out of the couple's love. Yes, we are wounded human beings and motivations are sometimes mixed. But at their best, couples want to conceive and bear a child as the fruit of their love. In God, our parent, this desire is perfect, and out of that perfect desire we are created.

When Catherine says God's wisdom created us, she means

the Spirit, the outpoured power of God's love. To drive home this ultimately indescribable reality, Catherine invites us to ponder God as Father-Parent bearing us from his womb. This metaphor tells us that we are a part of God, we are desired by God, our very existence and life come into existence out of the core of God. God-love desires our existence (see Pictorial Meditation 1).

Catherine asserts what sounds like an exaggeration, namely, that if God's love ceased to be, if it were to be withdrawn, we would cease to exist. But Catherine means this literally, and wise Christian thinkers from Augustine in the fifth century to Karl Rahner, the great late twentieth-century theologian, have come to a similar insight. Creation is filled with the presence of God, with the creative energy of God's love. Should that creative energy cease to exist, we and creation would somehow become a black hole; we would cease to be.

How can we respond to this gift of creation out of love? By intentionally having a close connection with God. For instance, in the second excerpt above, Catherine challenges us to imagine Jesus with breasts that bear milk. This daring feminine image of Jesus is a pictorial exhortation to develop a very close relationship with Jesus, who nourishes our capacity for love. We are invited to seek and take in that nourishment. Milk is the love of God offered through Jesus; and so, we are urged to attach ourselves to Jesus's milk-love-filled breasts. The pictorial message: in order to be nourished with Jesus's empowering (saving) love, we seek to be radically and foundationally close to Jesus. As mother milk (before formulas) is essential for the thriving of a child, closeness to Jesus is essential for the empowerment of our capacity to love.

We are invited to spend time "nourishing our souls," asking God to help us take in God's love and to allow that love to work within us. In one sense that love is already present because we are God's creation. But we must engage our free will and choose to open our consciousness—all that we are, desire, and feel—to God's action. There is a mystery about the fact that, on the one hand, God's gift of love holding us in being is free, given at creation; yet our free will—our capacity to consciously choose—has to be engaged (see chapter 9 on free will).

Catherine also invites us to choose and seek closeness to God because she knows what our faith teaches: while created out of love and for love, we are nevertheless vulnerable to sin, to the sin of self-centeredness (*disordered* focus on self), the opposite of love; we are wounded, imperfect persons. We need God's redemptive love given us in Jesus so that our woundedness and vulnerability to selfish self-love are transformed. We shall revisit the theme of our need for God because of our tendency to self-centeredness in several subsequent reflections, as it is one of Catherine's central themes.

Exercises

See instructions and guidelines for the different types of exercises in the introduction.

Grace: God, let me appreciate how much I need to be connected to your love in order to thrive as you want me to thrive.

Centering exercise

Phrase for monastic lectio: I am created out of love for love.

Imagination prayer exercises:

- Do Pictorial Meditation 1
- Picture a child in the mother's womb attached to the mother through the umbilical cord in order to receive oxygen and nourishment. Notice that the child thrives because of all that flows through that

umbilical cord. Now imagine God is the mother and you are attached to God through an umbilical cord, through which flows God's love. Watch your breathing as you allow this image to work in your consciousness. Be aware that when you use your will to pause and let God work within you, God is doing so, no matter what you feel or think. Make an act of faith that staying present to this image is a prayer that opens you to God's love and allows space for God to teach you in the depths of your consciousness that you are filled with God's love, tethered to that love.

- Imagine that you are sitting at Jesus's feet. Listen to Jesus tell you: "I want you to be a good, loving person; your life matters to me, what you do with your life matters to my creation; how you relate to other people affects others I love; so I want to help you grow in capacity to love. I want to do this because I want the best for you. When you function at your best, you thrive and others I love are benefitted."

  Listen to Jesus say this to you a few times. Ask for the grace to allow these words to touch you. Ask for the grace to truly believe these words apply to you and then repeat them a few more times. The goal is to allow the words to soak into your mind and heart, so that you grow in conviction and trust that God wants you to grow in capacity for love.

Pictorial Meditation 1

BIRTHED FROM GOD

For through love you were birthed from the womb of my Father who created you with his wisdom, and so through love you are held together for you are made of nothing else but love.

Letter 16

Take time to become centered. Focusing on this image, allow yourself to imagine being in the womb of God, a space of love where you are infused with God's life-giving love. Stay present to this image, watching it as you pay attention to your breath. When you lose your concentration, when you become distracted, return your attention to the image, saying to yourself: I am birthed from God, from love. Do this exercise for ten or more minutes if you can and pay attention to your inner experience. Depending on your inner experience, see what grace you wish to request from God. Do I desire the grace of inner certainty that I am birthed from God's love? Do I want to believe this can be so? Do I want to hold this belief close to consciousness so that I allow it to touch my daily experience? To offer me comfort? To offer me security? To bless me with peace through the assurance of being loved by God?

A brief meditation with this image can be an excellent daily exercise.

2

Recognizing God's Loving Presence

Letter 146—God's Love Is Like the Sea

Through such passionate love, I invite you to contemplate a peaceful, deep sea. I have discovered something new there—not that the sea is new—but I have a new feeling in my soul when contemplating the words, "God is love." As the mirror reflects a person's face, or the sun reflects light onto the earth, "God is love" mirrors in my soul that everything is pure love, that all is made only of love, which is why he says, "I am God-love."

Letter 127—Responding to God's Love

I, Catherine, useless servant, die of desire, returning from the depth of my soul where I experienced pain and weeping upon recognizing and tasting our ignorance and lukewarmness in not offering love to God, when with so much love he bestows so many graces upon us. And so, dearest brothers, don't be thankless and ungrateful, for the fountain of devotion within us could easily dry up. Oh, you who are lukewarm and negligent, awake from your perverse sleep!

Scripture

I the LORD will answer them.... I will make the wilderness a pool of water...so that all may see and know, all may consider and understand that the hand of the LORD has done this, the Holy One of Israel has created it. (Isa 41:18, 20)

Contemplation of nature can reveal God's creative love.

And a woman...brought an alabaster jar of ointment. She stood behind him...and began to bathe his feet with her tears and to dry them with her hair. Then she continued kissing his feet and anointing them with the ointment.... "Do you see this woman?" [Jesus says to the owner of the house]. "I entered your house; you gave me no water for my feet, but she has bathed my feet with her tears and dried them with her hair. You gave me no kiss, but from the time I came in she has not stopped kissing my feet. You did not anoint my head with oil, but she has anointed my feet with ointment....Hence she has shown great love." (Luke 7:37–38, 44–48)

Here Jesus shows appreciation of the woman's attention, gratitude, and expressions of love toward him and highlights the value of this gratitude.

Reflection

In moments of inner silence, when we tune in to our deepest self, a new window can open in our consciousness and suddenly we can see something in a new way. An inner light goes on and a new lens is placed in our consciousness so that reality comes alive with new meaning. This was Catherine's experience as she looked out to sea from the harbor of Pisa where the sea is peaceful, an expanse fading into the horizon. Connecting to her inner self, to the place in which the Spirit dwells, Catherine's view of the sea revealed something about God and God's love. God and God's love are as vast and infinite as the sea appears to be. With transformed consciousness, Catherine senses that God is telling her through this perception of the sea, "I am God-love." We too can internally see God's love present in creation and in other ordinary realities of daily life. We too can ask God to reveal God's love to us through ordinary human experience. We make this possible as we tune in to our inner selves, watching for a gift of light, for an opening in consciousness that discloses the God reality of our day-to-day experience.

Catherine speaks of "returning from the depth of my soul." To think about this passage and the many others in which Catherine uses the word *soul*, it is helpful to reimagine the word *soul*. Many of us have thought of the soul as a disembodied spiritual entity somehow residing in our body. Yet our soul is not separate from our body; rather, *soul* captures the spiritual dimension of our identity. While *identity* is an abstract idea, we can sense that *identity* captures our uniqueness; a uniqueness that is molded as we go through life. Because we are also spiritual beings, our unique identity is also a spiritual reality. That we can connect to God who exists in the spiritual realm tells us that we are also spiritual beings.

We can then imagine the soul as the spiritual dimension of our unique identity, the core of who we are that continues after death, after we are no longer bound by time and space. (My words are approximate, to help our imagination; I am not making a theological or philosophical argument.)

So, when Catherine says she returns from the depth of her soul, I picture her saying that she has tuned in with all her attention to her deepest inner self, her deepest unique identity, where God is present as the ground of the spiritual reality in which that identity is rooted. And in that depth of her consciousness, she encounters God with a fullness that reveals something profound about God's love. Catherine intuits that God cares that we recognize God's love and love God back. God is a person in Jesus and a personal being who enters into relationship with each of us, uniquely and personally, and wants to be loved back, as occurs in human relationships. When we love, we want to be loved back. Catherine grieves at how little we recognize this reality.

No wonder Catherine speaks of "returning" from a deep place in consciousness. For she has intuited a profound reality. She has learned, deeply and unmistakably, that God cares about our response to God's love.

Exercises

See instructions and guidelines for the different types of exercises in the introduction.

Grace: God, open my inner eyes to recognize you desire my response to your love.

Centering exercise

Phrase for monastic lectio: I know you love me. Give me the grace to love you back.

Imagination prayer exercises:

- Imagine that you are at the beach, sitting on the sand, in front of a calm sea with no waves. Look out over the sea and gaze at the horizon that makes the expanse of the sea seem infinite. Imagine that the sea is filled with God's love. Walk toward the water and start going into the sea. Imagine the water is warm and washes you with God's love as it bathes your legs and then your torso. As it does, feel God's love cleansing you, healing you, and renewing you. Note that this is unconditional. You only have to choose to enter into the water to receive the restorative power of the water-Love flowing over you. For as long as you can, stay present to this experience. Thank and praise God, the Spirit, or Jesus for the experience.
- Imagine you are watching a video of Catherine's experience described in Letter 127. She becomes quiet and centered. Then she has a powerful idea flow through her: God is sad when we don't respond to God's love, loving God back. Notice the effect of this startling insight on Catherine's face, her body. As you watch the video of her experience, become aware of yours. How are you reacting to her experience? What thoughts, what associations or images flow through your mind? What do you feel? What prayer emerges within you, that is, what do you want to say to God after watching Catherine's experience?

3

The Inner Cell

Letter 37—The Cell of Knowledge of Self and of God's Goodness

With desire to see you dwelling in the cell of knowledge of self and of the goodness of God within you. This cell is a dwelling place that persons carry with them wherever they go.

Letter 213—The Inner Cell Is a Home We Carry

She is able to pray anywhere because she carries with her the home where God dwells through grace, and where we pray. [This home] is the house of our soul, where holy, continuous desire always prays.

Scripture

And after he had dismissed the crowds, he went up the mountain by himself to pray. When evening came, he was there alone. (Matt 14:23)

And he said to his disciples, "Sit here while I go over there and pray." (Matt 26:36)

Jesus always carried within himself the trinitarian connection to the Father, and yet at times he found it necessary to be alone to tune in to this connection. In this passage we are told he went off to be alone close to where he ended his day of ministry. In other words, he sought solitude for communion with God where he was.

Reflection

One of Catherine's most central and important metaphors is that of the inner cell, a metaphor for which she uses many terms; for instance, there is the house of the soul, the cell of the soul, the cell of the side of Christ, and other similar terms. At one point, she says to one of her correspondents that God's goodness is "within you, cell" (Letter 73). This last expression highlights that in our deepest self, where our consciousness connects to spiritual reality, we are a cell, that is, a container or space in which we "enclose" or "hold" God's presence to us; in this space we experience God (see also chapter 6).

We can imagine the cell as the inner space that enables connection to God's love and to the knowledge of who we are reflected in that love. Let's look at a contemporary analogy to better understand this concept. We know that radio waves are all around us, but we need the right device to tune in to these waves and hear sound; without a radio—the correct device—the radio waves are there but we don't hear them. The inner cell is a metaphor for the device that receives and makes audible God's word to us about God's love and about ourselves. Thus, entering into the cell is equivalent to turning on the radio so that we can hear the sound. How do we "enter" the inner cell, or, as it were, turn on the radio? Through any form of practice that allows us to quiet our mind and consciousness and focus on God's presence within us and on our own reality in the light of God.

Catherine tells us the inner cell is a "home" we carry with us wherever we go. This is the case because God is always present to us; we can choose to quiet our mind and tune in to that presence wherever we are. Catherine is emphasizing two things here. One is that God's presence and our ability to know ourselves in the light of God is within us. We do not require a church or prayer corner, though these are helpful. We simply need to make the effort to find some quiet time anywhere we can settle down to tune in to our inner selves. Catherine also wishes to exhort her correspondent to consider that there is no excuse for not taking time for the practice of connecting to our inner self in order to tune in to God's presence.

Exercises

See instructions and guidelines for the different types of exercises in the introduction.

Grace: May I learn that I can always tune in to your presence which is within me.

Centering exercise

Phrase for monastic lectio: I am a home where you dwell. Or, I am a dwelling place for you, O God.

Imagination prayer exercises:

- Make a choice to spend time trying to *receive* God's love and communication. While set prayers are important, such as the rosary, or reciting the Divine Office, or quietly reading a piece of scripture, we need to learn to become receptive. To become receptive in prayer, we have to become like a device that receives input rather than one that emits. Picturing spending time in the cell as turning on the radio, imagine that you are the radio receiving the signals of God's love and God's transmission of God's word to you. Be attentive to the inner movements through which God communicates.

It is when in a receptive mode that we learn to recognize when a thought or an insight are God's communication to us in particular. We learn to identify when we feel consolation (sense of rightness, peace, hope) after talking to God about a problem or need; or to identify when we instead have experiences of desolation (distress, unease, lack of peace) after putting something in God's hands or asking God for guidance. Movements of consolation and desolation, a strong intuition floating through our minds, a strong "aha" experience, these can all be ways in which God's communication is received in the inner cell.

- Being in the inner cell—turning on the radio—may simply lead us to sense that God is acting within us, invisibly drawing us more deeply into God's presence. Here the communication is not an insight or inner word, but rather a sense of presence.
- Any form of centering prayer is also a way of spending time in the inner cell. (See Introduction for recommendations on centering prayer.) Take time to do a centering exercise for at least twenty minutes. It is normal that when we try to center, we become distracted with many thoughts (my worries, my to-do list, my current problems, my

next activity, my work, and so forth) and feelings (I'm mad at so and so; I'm anxious about...; I am hurting because...). As well, images file into our minds, from the last advertisement on the internet, to something we want to buy, to a scene from our daily life. As explained in the introduction, this is normal, and you should just return to your centering word or image. If soft, meditative music will help you to stay centered, include that in your exercise.

Notice that as time passes, despite distractions, you will become more able to tune in to your inner consciousness. Notice what that experience is like for you; try to articulate it and write it down in your journal. Writing out your experience will make it more concrete. Then take time to talk to God about this experience, thanking God for God's presence within you. Take time to say to yourself, "Yes, God is always with me. I carry God's presence within me."

4

Two Cells in One

Letter 49—Two Cells: Knowing God, Knowing Self

The other room [the inner room], you create spiritually and always carry with you. This is the cell of the true knowledge of yourself, where you find knowledge of God's goodness within you. [These two forms of knowledge] give you two cells in one; when you dwell in one of these it is important for you to dwell in the other at the same time so that the soul does not become arrogant and muddled [spiritually troubled]. If you dwell [only] in knowledge of yourself, you would become muddled, and if you dwell only in knowledge of God, you would become proud. So the two forms of knowledge should season each other and form a whole. In this way you will reach perfection.

Letter 51—Know God, Know Self in God

For truth exists when the person knows himself and understands the goodness of God within him. If the person knows only himself, or if he should want to know God without knowing himself, his knowledge would not be founded on truth; nor would the person receive the benefit that he should garner from knowledge of self. He would lose rather than gain, for from self-knowledge alone he would only garner spiritual troubles and anxiety, which would dry up the soul; and if he continued in this state without other alternatives, he would become despairing. And should he want to know God without knowing himself, he would reap the stinking fruit of considerable arrogance, which nurtures pride; and arrogance and pride feed on each other. It is important, then, that the light [of understanding] gaze upon truth, seasoning knowledge of self with knowledge of God, and knowledge of God with knowledge of self.

Scripture

They show that what the law requires is written in their hearts, to which their own conscience also bears witness. (Rom 2:15)

Paul tells us that we carry within ourselves the capacity to know God as God's law written in our hearts and to know about ourselves through the movements of our conscience.

Reflection

What do we seek to experience in the inner cell? We seek to know God and to know ourselves in the light of God. These two forms of knowledge are the central dynamic, the central practice of a spiritual path, according to Catherine of Siena.

First, let's reflect on what she means by "knowledge." Knowledge here doesn't mean acquiring information that feeds our brain. It is not a matter of learning truths as facts to which we assent. That, for Catherine, would be only a small beginning. The knowledge to which she refers is that which we learn in a heartfelt way with the core of our being. It is the intuitive recognition of reality that emerges into our awareness when our inner consciousness is tuned in to God. Such emerging recognition entails new insights, new perspectives, or greater clarity about an issue in our lives.

Knowledge of self means awareness of two important realities about ourselves, which might seem contradictory. Because we are created in the image of God, we have great capacity for goodness. We are capable of care for others, of sacrifice for others, of heroism, of faithful commitment to those we love, of faithful commitment to follow God. At the same time, we have a shadow side, a foundational tendency toward self-centeredness, root of all sinfulness. We can be uncaring, unfaithful, self-preoccupied, and certainly capable of hurting and harming others. We are always vulnerable to forgetting God, to being unfaithful to God's values and God's best desires for our lives. So, knowledge of self entails conscious recognition of these two foundational aspects of who we are.

Knowledge of God involves the gift of internalizing how much we are loved and valued by God. This includes the experience of God as caring, God as personally interested in us, God as healing, God as guide, God as source of strength. It is the experience of God's unconditional mercy and unconditional acceptance of who we are in all our imperfection.

By the metaphor of two cells in one, Catherine tells us that the inner experience of knowing self, especially being conscious of our woundedness and sinfulness, must occur in the context of knowing ourselves unconditionally accepted and loved by God. For just focusing on our faults and failures without the mercy and comfort of knowing ourselves unconditionally loved by God is not constructive for our growth and transformation. On the other hand, if we were to bask in feeling loved by God but were not aware of our shadow side, we would fall into pride or self-complacency and even a false self-assurance. If we focus only on experiences of consolation, never troubling ourselves with consciousness of our faults, we can easily become self-righteous.

Thus, Catherine emphasizes the importance of having these two forms of inner experience, these two forms of inner knowledge, in synchronicity, concurrently; these two forms of intuitive understanding must be two intimately related parts of a whole.

Note that when Catherine refers to "perfection" she means the transformation into persons capable of love through the process of receiving God's transforming love as we grow in knowledge of God and self.

Exercises

See instructions and guidelines for the different types of exercises in the introduction.

Grace: God, let me acknowledge my woundedness, my unloving and selfish behaviors, while I also learn of your unconditional, merciful love.

Centering exercise

Phrase for monastic lectio: Your love compassionately touches all my woundedness and sin.

Imagination prayer exercises:

- Once you are quieted down, ask God for the grace to remember times when you felt blessed by God or touched by his grace (ways in which we feel loved). Perhaps you had a sense of God's unconditional forgiveness, or you had a sense of comfort, peace, and/or joy during a liturgy or prayer service, or perhaps you have experienced an answer to prayer that left you with deep gratitude, or maybe you have felt healing of emotional distress. Once you are able to connect to such memories of God's blessings and love, ask God to help you become aware of some dimension of your shadow side. Allow yourself to tune in, without avoidance, to whatever the Spirit sends into your consciousness. Then surrender this knowledge about yourself to God's merciful, healing love. This exercise is meant to help you hold in consciousness experiences of God's blessings and love at the same time that you tune in to aspects of yourself that need transformation.

- A continuation or follow-up to the above exercise is to review your experience and see if you notice times when you have been caught up in feeling guilty about a choice or behavior; or times when you have obsessed about a repeated failing on your part or something that has left you feeling ashamed or embarrassed. Notice if when quiet, or as you go about your day, these negative emotions and thoughts about yourself pull you down, or leave you stressed, or sad. Getting caught up in such negative scripts about ourselves is a large part of what Catherine means by "becoming muddled."

  Or perhaps you automatically avoid these negative feelings. Some may turn to distractions or escapes, some even to addictive behaviors, in order to avoid these uncomfortable inner feelings.

As you recall such troubling experiences, turn your attention to God, and tell God you hand over the feeling, the memory, the experience. If you experience remorse, hand that over to Jesus as well, asking for mercy and grace to improve. Ask for the grace to realize that God loves you unconditionally, no matter what failings, faults, and disordered behavior you may engage in. Ask for the grace to learn to love and accept yourself with your woundedness and failings as Jesus does. Notice what you experience.

5

The Cell as Well: *I-Am-Not*—God IS

Letter 41—Cell as Well

"Most beloved children, if you wish to find and experience the reward of living in my will, always dwell in the cell of your soul." [Words Catherine sensed Jesus spoke to her. She then continues in her own words.] This cell is a well which contains both soil and water—where the soil can be understood to be our moral weakness, that *we-are-not*; when we recognize *we-are-not*, we also realize that our being comes from God. Oh ineffable, passionate Love! I can see that the soil has been found, and the living water reached. That is, the genuine knowledge of God's benevolent and true will, which desires nothing more than that we be made holy.

Let us then enter into the depth of this well; for if we dwell there, we will inevitably come to know ourselves and God's goodness. As we learn that *we-are-not*, we grow in humility so that we enter meekly into that open heart that warms and consumes and which is also like a window that never closes yet through which one cannot leave....This is my desire, to see you in this dwelling, becoming transformed; and not just you, but all other persons.

Letter 73—Balanced Knowledge of God and Self

I would like you to be aware of your negligence and ignorance and that *you-are-not,* but I do not want you to experience this because of darkness and inner trouble; I want you to learn this through God's infinite goodness, which is within you....For, knowledge of weaknesses should be seasoned with the condiment of hope in God's mercy.

Scripture

David was stricken to the heart....David said to the LORD, "I have sinned greatly in what I have done. But now, O LORD, I pray you take away the guilt of your servant: for I have done very foolishly." [Through the prophet Gad, God sent a response to David.] Thus says the LORD: Three things I offer you; choose one of them, and I will do it.... David said to Gad, "I am in great distress; let us fall into the hand of the LORD, for his mercy is great; but let me not fall into human hands." (2 Sam 24:10, 12, 14)

David has acted without God's guidance and thus ended up in great trouble. David recognizes he has acted without God, forgetting *he-is-not*. He realizes that anything coming from God's hand, even a punishment, is better than being left to his own devices and to the fate at the hands of his human enemies. So, David repents of acting without seeking God's will or God's help. Though king and absolute ruler, David learned God IS and *he-is-not*.

> *For by grace you have been saved through faith, and this is not your own doing; it is the gift of God—not the result of works, so that no one may boast. For we are what he has made us, created in Christ Jesus for good works. (Eph 2:8–10)*

Our capacity for goodness is the fruit of grace, of God's transforming life given to us in Christ Jesus. Learning that our capacity for goodness is radically rooted in grace is learning that *we-are-not* and God IS.

Reflection

Since knowledge of God and self are such key aspects of Catherine's spirituality, we deepen our understanding of these through her metaphor of the cell as a well. We imagine a well that has been stopped up by mud, so one must dig through the mud to get to the water. Digging through the mud is the process of coming to recognize that *we-are-not*. Catherine came up with this phrase reflecting on God's words to Moses, "I AM WHO I AM" (Exod 3:14). That is, God is life, God is love, God is existence; and *we-are-not* in that we owe our existence to God; we need God so that we can become capable of the love for which we were created. The words *we-are-not* represent Catherine's mystically acquired wisdom regarding how much we need God. It is not a statement that we lack worth, for the opposite is true from God's perspective.

Catherine tells us that through knowledge of self we learn humility. Humility here means the grace to recognize that we are not sufficient onto ourselves but need God's grace. Note that humility does not mean being self-effacing. Catherine's authoritative way of writing to the highest civil and religious authorities and of telling people of all walks of life how to follow God, and how they were failing, was hardly self-effacing. But she deeply knew that her authority and effectiveness came from God.

Perhaps in theory we can say we know we need God; yet, recognizing this experientially can be altogether different. Acquiring such experiential knowledge often entails arduously "digging through the mud" of Catherine's metaphorical well. We learn we need God when we recognize that our willpower and efforts are not enough to overcome our self-centeredness and all the ways in which we fail to be the persons capable of love that God wants us to be. We experience the grace of humble self-knowledge when we feel in our bones that without God's grace we keep repeating our disordered behaviors; we keep failing to live up to our potential; we keep being lazy about our spiritual practices; we keep up our unkind behaviors or nasty gossiping; we keep distorting the truth to benefit ourselves. When in the midst of such self-awareness we perceive God touching us and helping us, we learn we need God.

We also learn how much we need God when we must come to terms with serious suffering, loss, or limitation, and we recognize that without grace we would despair or become despondent or chronically angry and bitter. We experience our need for God when we can forgive a great wrong only through God's grace; or when we can accept unchangeable situations after prayer.

Catherine's metaphor of the well pictures the water found after digging through the mud as living water or God's empowering life and love. The living water we find is God's action in our lives to empower our best self. Living water is God's transforming grace. Living water is God's love enabling us to live constructively despite, and through suffering and loss of meaning.

Catherine layers her metaphors to emphasize her point; in the above excerpt she tells us that finding living water after digging through the mud is also like entering into the open heart of Christ which is like a window always open. The open heart of Christ is God's love always ready to receive us. God's readiness to receive us is never "closed."

When in our weakness and need we enter into Christ's heart, that is, we ask for God's help, and then notice improvement in our capacity to cope or in our ability to live in a loving, constructive way, we learn that God is love; that God is redemptive power; that God is comfort; that God is source of meaning in suffering. We learn that God is the ultimate person who cares about us and the foundational source of assistance for the living of life with meaning and peace. This is the meaning of learning that God IS.

Exercises

See instructions and guidelines for the different types of exercises in the introduction.

Grace: Give me the grace to recognize that *I-am-not,* that my being and capacity for goodness comes from you, my God.

Centering exercise

Phrase for monastic lectio: "God's benevolent and true will...desires nothing more than that we be made holy" (From Letter 41 above).

Imagination prayer exercises:

- Reread the story of David above. After becoming centered, ask the Spirit to help you remember when your story has been like David's story, that is, a story of acting without guidance from God or of acting without reference to your most centered or ethical self. Remember this episode of your life. How can you learn from it as David learned? Can you relive the memory imagining how it would have played out with God's help? Take time to see what intuition emerges. Listen to God invite you to live an experience like this in a different manner, namely, after consulting God and your most ethical self. Notice that God helps you learn how to live differently, even as God values you and accepts you. Knowing God's unconditional acceptance helps us to review choices we have made with less defensiveness and to learn from experience. Engage in a dialogue with God about your experience and insight.

- A similar exercise: After centering, ask yourself, in what ways have you been trying to "dig through the mud," that is, trying to save yourself or to deal with a difficult life reality or loss without seeking God's help? Be as inwardly still as possible and let the Spirit bring into your consciousness what you most need to notice at this time of prayer. Keeping in mind Catherine's metaphor of the living water, God who IS (love, mercy, healing love, the whisperer of the right discernment, and so forth), ask God for help, trusting that God will assist you and empower you.

6

The Cell: Going to Bed

Letter 73—The Cell and the Bed

[What do] you do when you go into your cell at night to go to sleep? First you reach your cell [bedroom], and once inside, you see your bed. You clearly know that you need the cell [in order to sleep], but your eye and your desire focus on your bed, where you find rest. You should act in a similar manner when you reach the cell of self-knowledge where I want you to open the eye of understating through affective love. Enter the cell and go to bed, where you will find God's benevolent goodness, which is within you, cell. You will see clearly that your being was granted to you through grace and not out of obligation.

For you see my daughter, this bed is covered with a red bedspread dyed in the blood of the sacrificed Lamb totally given for us; rest there and never leave. Notice that you have no cell without a bed nor a bed without a cell. Fatten your soul on this goodness of God, because whoever is in this bed is richly fed, as this bed holds the table, the food, and the waiter; that is, the Father is the table, the Son is the food, and the Holy Spirit waits on you and makes of himself a bed for you....And so, I beg you, for the love of Christ crucified, remain in this loving, glorious bed.

Scripture

God teaches Elijah how to listen to God's voice:

"Go out and stand on the mountain before the LORD, for the LORD is about to pass by." Now there was a great wind,... but the LORD was not in the wind; and after the wind, an earthquake, but the LORD was not in the earthquake; and after the earthquake a fire, but the LORD was not in the fire; and after the fire the sound of sheer silence. (1 Kings 19:11–12)

In the silence Elijah heard the voice of God. Thus, God teaches Elijah that God is heard, recognized, experienced when outer reality is quiet, similar to going into a quiet bedroom and lying still in bed.

You prepare a table before me in the presence of my enemies; you anoint my head with oil; my cup overflows. (Ps 23:5)

The Psalmist saw God, Yahweh, as setting a table, a metaphor for offering protection and all needed grace.

Reflection

Catherine tells us that entering into the cell of self-knowledge is like going to bed at night (in the case of a monk or nun). First, we enter a bedroom where we have silence and solitude, and then we go to bed, which symbolizes entering further into inner silence. In this case, Costanza, the nun to whom Catherine is writing, should go into her cell (her bedroom), a place for silence and solitude in the life of a medieval nun. Having achieved outer silence and solitude, Costanza now has the space to enter into the inner experience of knowing herself and God—going to bed.

Catherine underscores that Costanza should go to bed—not just into her cell—to stress that outer silence and solitude together with relaxation and rest from all inner noise and activity are critical to consciously encounter God. Silence and solitude (the physical cell) are a beginning, but they are not enough. For we could be in silence and solitude and remain inwardly "busy" with thoughts and plans, or nurturing resentments or hurts, or preoccupied with ourselves without reference to God's presence within.

The cell, as we saw in other meditations, is the space of consciousness in which we encounter and sense God's presence. In Catherine's layered metaphor, this means we are ourselves a "cell," as Catherine writes to Costanza, saying, *"which is within you, cell."* That is, who we are is a vessel for God's presence, as our inner consciousness is a "space" for encounter with God.

Catherine often offers layers of meaning that are not logically related. We must let go of logic and instead attend to her metaphors as we would to images painted in words by a poem; we allow images to evoke an experience. In the above excerpt, the bed creatively becomes a table where God can "fatten" our soul, feeding us richly (an image from Catherine's familiarity with raising sheep, as her father was in the wool business). At this table we encounter God as Trinity. God the Father provides the table and sets it, Jesus is the food, and the Holy Spirit the waiter. God is source of all that fattens our soul in that God is love and transforming grace. Jesus is the love and grace of the Father that we can literally eat in communion; and the Holy Spirit is God's presence guiding us and inspiring us to seek God and God's love. Notice this metaphor is one of service, of free gift. The table set for us to eat is a free offering of sustenance. God desires so much to feed us that God sets the table; and God wants to make it easy for us to eat by having God's Son be the waiter, the person who serves us our food. As if this were not enough, God provides the Spirit to guide us to sit down and focus on taking in the food being offered. So, when we enter into inner silence, we create space to become aware, through the Spirit, of God's desire to nurture us with transforming love.

The red bedspread is another layer of Catherine's metaphor. It is a symbol of Jesus's blood, which means the life Jesus gave for our salvation; it is God's love given through Jesus in his crucifixion and then as food for us in the Eucharist. (See chapters 14, 15, and 16 on Jesus's blood as the life of God.)

In short, through the metaphors of a table and a bedspread, Catherine seeks to open our imagination to visualize how God seeks to offer us transforming love and food for our spiritual growth and for the living of life in the most meaningful, God-centered way.

Exercises

See instructions and guidelines for the different types of exercises in the introduction.

Grace: Teach me that you set a table for me to partake of the nourishing food of your unconditional love. Give me the grace to show up at that table every day.

Centering exercise

Phrase for monastic lectio: I want to be fed at your table.

Imagination prayer exercises:

- Imagine walking into a quiet bedroom where you can be alone. Imagine that you settle into bed in order to be extra relaxed and attentive to inner experience. What else do you need to become inwardly quiet? Perhaps playing meditative music or a recording of sounds to quiet your mind, or saying the rosary, or reciting a psalm in a repetitive way. Imagine that Jesus is there to help you settle into bed in a comfortable way, to help you relax. Then, imagine that Jesus brings a red bedspread to keep you warm, and this bedspread emits Jesus's saving life. Take time to imagine this or something similar and see what happens. What emerges into your consciousness? What conversation do you want to have with Jesus? Or perhaps you just want to lie in the bed allowing the emissions of healing life from the bedspread to penetrate you. The latter would be a contemplative, centering exercise.
- Imagine that God invites you to sit at a table. Notice that Jesus is the waiter-attendant. He could minister to you through anointing, as in the psalm, or through giving you bread and wine, his saving life. Do you need to be fed? Or do you need to be "anointed with oil," that is, tended to, healed, or touched in some way by the oil of Jesus's loving and transforming care for you? As you do this exercise, pay attention to any memory or feeling that is surfacing into your consciousness. Allow Jesus to be the "waiter" that feeds you or the attendant that anoints you in your need.

7

We Are a Tree of Love

Letter 363—Tree Planted in the Soil of Humility

[You should not be like a leaf that can be swept away.] Rather, you should be like a tree that is planted in the grounded soil of true humility, so that the wind of pride cannot harm the tree of your soul. For your soul is a tree of love, created by God for love and made of love; and she cannot live from anything other than love—be it holy love or selfish self-love. If the tree is planted high up on the mountain of pride, selfish self-love destroys and kills the life of grace; [up there] it is blown by gusts of wind blowing in multiple directions, damaging it... its fruit fall to the ground....Oh how glorious is the tree of our soul when it is so lovingly planted following the humility of the Immaculate Lamb from whom we received life; he is a sun emitting grace and mercy.

Letter 185—Soil of Knowledge of Self

I wish to see you a fruitful tree full of sweet, ripe fruit, planted in rich soil—the soil of true knowledge of self; for if not rooted in this soil the tree would become dry and would bear no fruit. The tree's fruit dries up; it cannot remain lush, because whoever cares for self with selfish self-love is someone who has wicked pride living within, and such pride is the beginning and source of all evil.

Scripture

They are the shoot that I planted, the work of my hands, so that I might be glorified. (Isa 60:21)

God tells Isaiah that God's people are like a shoot, a plant created by God—the work of God's hands—so we assume the shoot is planted in just the right place.

But I am like a green olive tree in the house of God. I trust in the steadfast love of God forever and ever. (Ps 52:8)

Those who are in relationship with God are like flourishing olive trees—trees especially prized in the land of the Psalmist.

Reflection

Through the metaphor of the well-planted tree, Catherine offers us another approach to visualizing that we are created out of love in order to love. Here Catherine expands on this teaching, telling us that because loving is inherent to our nature, we will love, desire, or get attached, either in self-centered ways or in ways congruent with Jesus's example of love. In other words, humans will always find something or somebody toward which to direct desire. The goal of transformation is to have that drive directed to that which is congruent with God's love.

When Catherine repeats through many metaphors and in many words that we are made for love, she is *not* referring to the emotional feeling of attachment. She doesn't mean the *feeling* of attachment to my spouse or my child, or my religious order, although such emotions are indeed a fruit of love. Catherine means by love the willingness, desire, and perseverance to engage with the reality of others. This is Catherine's overarching message, that love has to do with first noticing and recognizing the other, then recognizing what the other needs, and third, in an ordered way, giving of ourselves for the good of that other. The love for which we are created is this capacity and not an emotion or attachment, though, again, such emotions are part of some forms of love.

Who is "the other"? Most obviously it is my family members, those I live with and those who form my extended family. It is those I work with or those for whom I work. "The other" can be a group of people such as a church group to which I belong, a group with whom I play an instrument, a set of friends with whom I engage in a sport. The other can also be impersonal. It is any level of community, whether I am involved in it or not. For instance, the town or the country I live in are "others" I should care about, even if I am not a government employee (we will return to this idea). The other is certainly the organization for which I work or the school I attend or the school my children attend. It is, as Pope Francis has told us, the environment, our common home.

Catherine tells us that the opposite of love is selfish self-love or self-centeredness. We are all, to some extent, self-centered. Self-centeredness can be expressed in self-absorption, in self-preoccupation, in being wrapped up in ourselves so that we don't notice the other and what they need, or we barely notice, or we notice and return to our own self-interests. We are self-centered when we give priority to ourselves at times when it would be appropriate to give attention, time, and energy to another. Or when we are so focused on our own views and on the lenses through which we look at life, that we are unable to step outside of our own standpoints to see the other in their uniqueness or their need, which may not be ours. We are self-centered when we hurt others out of lack of empathy, when we lie to benefit ourselves or protect ourselves, when we prefer our wealth to honesty, when we prefer power to the good of our family or job, when we treat others in demeaning or entitled ways. We counter self-centeredness when we learn to focus our attention on the other and ask, what does he or she or they need from me at this moment, how can I contribute or give of myself to this other or others at this moment in time? If the other is in distress, what are they experiencing? What do they need from me? Notice that we often assume others need and want what we would need or want.

Let's look at some examples about caring for more impersonal "others." To what extent do I care about our common home and respond to Pope Francis's call to care for the earth? While not all of us are called to be environmental activists, all of us can trouble ourselves to deposit trash in the correct recycling bins. We can all ask ourselves if we unnecessarily waste water or electricity. Self-focus in this case means we simply don't care about these important issues; we don't recycle, or we waste water without awareness of the effect on our common home. To what extent am I attentive to issues in my community that would benefit from my participation? Voting in elections is one way of caring for the good of our broader community. We can trouble ourselves to become knowledgeable about candidates and issues so that we can make informed choices. In the case of impersonal others, recognizing what is needed requires that we leave our self-complacency and our preoccupation only with our own concerns; it requires that we look outside the narrow prism of that which most interests us or our individual affairs; it requires that we focus on the communities in which we live and the organizations that affect our lives.

At the same time, in the twenty-first century we would say that it is also healthy to care about oneself and to care for one's responsibilities and priorities. It is healthy to have compassion for our woundedness and neediness and spend time and energy on self-care. There are times when it is healthy to set limits regarding engagement in the needs of others or in commitments to causes, as the life realities and circumstances of each of our lives affect what and how much we can give. I believe Catherine would advise careful discernment, with the help of the Spirit, to distinguish between healthy self-care and disordered self-centeredness.

Exercises

See instructions and guidelines for the different types of exercises in the introduction.

Grace: My God, show me a specific instance of my self-centeredness. May I see it through your compassionate eyes.

Centering exercise

Phrase for monastic lectio: I am a tree of love.

Imagination prayer exercises:

- Catherine offers us the image of the tree planted in the soil of humility; humility is accurate knowledge of ourselves, which includes recognizing when and how we are self-centered. Holding in your mind this image of the soil of humility, imagine that you have been given a small fruit tree; that you need to find the right soil in which to plant it. Notice the importance of the soil for the well-being of the plant. Without soil, most plants won't grow; in fact, they will die. The quality of the soil is crucial. So, you look for soil rich in nutrients that nurture the growth of the tree, nutrients that make it possible for the tree to flower and bear fruit. Periodically you fertilize the soil. You wouldn't plant your new tree in old used up soil that has been sapped of nutrients; such soil would barely keep the tree alive.

With awareness of the importance of the soil for the tree to flourish, ask the Spirit to help you see how this metaphor applies to you today. What is equivalent to good soil for planting your tree? For instance, what practices would help you grow in knowledge of yourself? Do you need to take stock each night? Do you want to spend one prayer period a month asking for grace to know yourself as God knows you? Do you want to ask others in your personal life or in your faith community for feedback on yourself? Take time to see what emerges in your consciousness as you switch focus from the image of the fruit tree to yourself. The goal of metaphors is to stir our feelings, our intuitions, to open space for grace to work. Is there new understanding, new insight emerging within you? Is there something about your life and reality emerging into your consciousness? Let the Spirit guide your prayer with whatever emerges.

- Another approach to this theme: After centering yourself, keep in your awareness the tree of love.

To flourish, it must be planted in the right soil, and this soil includes awareness of those areas of our life where we put ourselves at the center of reality to the exclusion of the realities of those others who are or should be part of our life. Ask the Spirit to help you review your current life in these terms. Through the Spirit's inspiration, become aware of an area in your life where you have been self-absorbed, or a way in which you are behaving selfishly or uncaringly in a relationship. Or perhaps you notice how you could contribute to a cause in your community, but you are resisting doing so. Dialogue with Jesus about your new awareness. What do you need from God? Ask for this grace.

8

Fruit of a Well-Planted Tree

Letter 252—Gregory XI Should Be Lovingly Rooted

I want you [Pope Gregory XI] to be a tree of love grafted onto the Word-love, Christ crucified, a tree whose roots are planted in deep humility for the honor of God and the salvation of your sheep. If you become a tree of love, lovingly rooted, you will find in yourself, tree of love, the fruits of patience and fortitude on the top of the tree, and in the middle perseverance with its crown. You will find peace, stillness, and consolation in suffering, as you experience being conformed [through suffering] to Christ crucified.

Letter 133—The Tree and Its Flowers

My dearest daughter, if the gardener, free will, plants where she should, namely, in the soil of true humility—for it [the tree] should not be planted on the hill of pride but in the valley of humility—then the tree will produce fragrant flowers, namely, the virtues, and, most specially, it will produce the greatest flower, the glory and praise of God's name. And then all her acts and virtues will become sweet fruit and flowers perfumed with this scent [of the glory and praise of God's name]. This is the flower, my dearest daughter, that makes our virtues bloom.

Letter 363—Tree Protected between Mountains

[What keeps the tree rooted in the soil of humility?] I'll tell you. The hatred and dislike of our selfish sensuality [that is, *disordered* seeking of any form of pleasure, such as luxury, power, status, delectable foods, sexual experience]. In this way the tree will be located between two strong mountains, that is, the virtues of fortitude and true patience. These two can tolerate all kinds of contrary winds....And so the virtues are protected and these fruit ripen. So, then the person will teach her neighbor with her wisdom and words through perfumed flowers, that is, through righteous thoughts the result of right-ordered judgments; the person becomes able to discern in herself and her neighbor the tender will of God, who wants nothing but our good.

Scripture

Their delight is the law of the LORD, and on his law they meditate day and night. They are like trees planted by streams of water, which yield their fruit in its season and their leaves do not wither. (Ps 1:2–3)

The Psalmist celebrates those committed to following God and God's guidance. Such people are like trees that are well planted: in this case, in a place where they will receive sufficient water.

Having been destined according to the purpose of him who accomplishes all things according to his counsel and will, so that we, who were the first to set our hope on Christ, might live for the praise of his glory. (Eph 11: 12)

Praising God's glory, which is living out our redeemed potential according to God's will, is one of the fruits for which we are created.

Reflection

In these excerpts, through the metaphor of the tree, Catherine underscores the importance of close adherence to Jesus in order for our tree to remain solidly planted and be a thriving tree of love on which bears fine fruit.

In Letter 252 above, Catherine exhorts Gregory XI to be *grafted* onto Christ crucified. If not grafted onto Jesus Savior, the pope will be unable to perform his mission as desired by God. When a plant is grafted onto another, the grafted piece begins to receive sap and nutrients from the main plant. So, Jesus crucified—addressed here by Catherine as the "Word-love"—is the main tree and we are the grafted plant. This metaphor about being grafted onto Jesus suggests that without closeness to Jesus we would not have the nutrients we need to thrive; we would be like a plant without roots that would die if not grafted onto a living, well-planted tree. To be a living tree, we need a deep connection to God's sap of life and love. This intimate connection allows us to live humbly, that is, aware of our need for God and committed to actively seeking God's help. And this awareness and openness to God's help significantly enables us to live according to God's love.

The well-planted or properly grafted tree bears fine fruit. In the letter to Gregory XI, Catherine names the fruit of such a tree in terms of the virtues, namely, patience and fortitude, consolation in suffering, peace and stillness. When we have a spiritual life that fosters and nurtures closeness to Jesus, we receive the grace to live through difficulties and suffering with strength (fortitude) and meaning rather than turning in on ourselves or hurting others out of our suffering; we receive strength to deal with the ordinary and extraordinary tasks and duties of daily life; we are able to persevere in our spiritual practices without laziness or laxness or without being distracted by daily occurrences. And we receive one of the most valuable fruits of a spiritual life, peace. Abiding inner peace is a gift that exists despite the struggles of daily life or times of suffering, confusion, and other forms of distress. The foregoing fruits, strength, patience, and peace, give us the centeredness and strength to live with fidelity according to our highest values and with the perseverance and life energy to care for the good of the other.

In Letter 133 Catherine's metaphorical language about the fruit of the tree is particularly illuminating. The flower that precedes the fruit is "the greatest flower, the glory and praise of God's name" so that all that we do—the fruit—is "perfumed with the scent" of the glory and praise of God's name. This metaphor is saying that when our life is lived rooted in true humility—recognition that we need God—and attached to the saving power of God as nutrient, then what we do and choose is more likely to be in tune with God's will, which is always centered on love.

In letter 363 Catherine explains that when living a life of honesty regarding one's vulnerabilities and sinfulness—indicating that we recognize our need for God—the fruits we produce are thoughts and desires increasingly congruent with the wisdom of God. As we go about our life, if our actions and engagement with others are congruent with the wisdom of God, we give witness to God's love and truth, we bear the fruit of being representatives of God's care for us and of God's values for the way in which life should be lived. This wisdom also reflects Catherine's teaching on discernment, namely, that as we are transformed through the ongoing practice of knowing our need for God and allowing God's love and mercy to touch us, we become more and more capable of acting according to God's will, which is also God's desire for our well-being and that of those around us.

Exercises

Grace: May I grow in becoming grafted onto Jesus, my Savior.

Centering exercise

Phrase for monastic lectio: I plant my tree of love by the living water.

Imagination prayer exercises:

- This exercise aims to help you get in touch with the fruit of the tree of love in your own life. According to Catherine's two excerpts above, the fruits of the well-planted tree of love are patience, strength, courage, perseverance, peace, and consolation in the midst of suffering, and the capacity to discern correctly God's will for ourselves and our neighbor. After centering yourself, ask the Spirit to surface into your consciousness one or two of these virtues—qualities of personality—on which to focus this prayer period. Notice concrete ways in which you have or lack these characteristics. Or perhaps you notice how you have grown in these qualities as a result of your spiritual journey. What dialogue with God do these reflections inspire? Take time to engage in speaking with Jesus. Or perhaps you see how much you need one or another of these qualities, in which case focus on asking God for the grace of acquiring them.

- Imagine you have in your living room a bouquet of fragrant flowers. Imagine you sit in this room, close your eyes, and focus on this fragrance. Notice that the fragrance reaches you and delights you; it has an impact on you. Focusing on this visualization, notice that God calls you to be such a fragrance for others through your witness to them. How do we witness? We witness through the way in which we live our life, through the way in which we behave at work, in our community, with our friends. How we live and how we treat others out of a place of transformation in capacity to love is the best witness. Take time to dialogue with Jesus about whatever insights, questions, or petitions emerge from these reflections.
- You might be struggling with how to be a witness for God's values in a particular situation. Bringing into awareness the metaphor of the fragrant flowers, ask the Spirit to inspire you. Ask, how can I be

a fragrance for others? Listen to any inner nudge or inspiration that represents God's guidance. God will always wish you to be fragrance for others out of your unique identity and reality. Dialogue with God about your insights.

Pictorial Meditation 2

WELL-PLANTED TREE

I wish to see you a fruitful tree full of sweet, ripe fruit, planted in rich soil—the soil of true knowledge of self. (Letter 185) Then the tree will produce fragrant flowers, namely, the virtues, and, most specially, it will produce the greatest flower, the glory and praise of God's name. And then all her acts and virtues will become sweet fruit and flowers perfumed with this scent [of the glory and praise of God's name].

Letter 363

The roots of this tree are vibrant and alive, planted in a rich soil that is also dynamic and full of an energy that sustains the life of the tree flowing through its branches, making fine flowers possible. This rich soil is the practice of knowing ourselves accurately, especially recognizing how much we need God (humility). After centering yourself, focus on this image. Notice the violet nutrients taken up from the soil through the vibrant roots; these nutrients then flow through the branches and empower the emergence of fine flowers. The nutrient of knowledge of ourselves before God is as foundational to our capacity to love as a nutrient-rich soil is to the tree's well-being and its ability to thrive and produce flowers and fruit. As you are centered in meditation focused upon this image, allow yourself to pay attention to the reality that, like this tree, you can bear the glorious fruit of love when you allow the living nutrients of being connected to God to reach your needs, faults, and vulnerabilities.

Ask yourself the following questions and allow answers to emerge from within you, without forcing answers from the top of your head. Be still and be patient in allowing answers to emerge. Look at the marvelous flowers of this tree, beautiful and full of the light and energy of love. Do I want to be a tree of love that bears the fruit and flowers of love? Do I desire to have that violet nutrient of knowledge of self flow through me? If I do, I take time and space to be drawn in by the image of the tree and to allow new awareness of self or God that the Spirit sends into my consciousness. As this meditation proceeds, you may connect to a heartfelt desire to know yourself more fully as you are seen by God. Thank God for this grace and for whatever graces you receive from this meditation.

9

Free Will and Love

Letter 133—The Tree and Free Will

My dearest daughter, *if the gardener, free will,* plants where she should…

Letter 113—The Heart-Sponge and Free Will

For, when in love with divine love, our heart acts like a sponge that draws water into itself. Of course, even if the sponge is ready to absorb water, it will not do so if it is not placed in water. This is how I want you to imagine the readiness of our heart which is made to love and ready to love. Our heart—though made for and readied to love—will never fill with grace unless the light of understanding and the *hand of free will* lift it into the fire of divine love; for when united with divine love our heart will always be filled. Which is why I said that through love and with love, love is brought forth.

Letter 374—Chain mail of Free Will

I want your safety to be in Christ, loving Jesus. He has clothed us in the sturdiest clothing possible, which is love covered with the *chain mail of free will*; you have the choice of fully buckling up this armor or of loosening it. If someone wants to remove this clothing of love, they are free to do so; and if someone wants to keep it on, they can do so as well. Think about this, dearest father, the first clothing we had was love, since we were created out of sheer love, in the image and likeness of God; and so, persons cannot live without love, as they are made of nothing else but love.

Scripture

For freedom Christ has set us free. Stand firm, therefore, and do not submit again to a yoke of slavery. (Gal 5:1)

Paul tells the Galatians that Christ has set us free from sin so that we can choose God and what is according to God's love. Free will is a potential of persons that must be made operative by God's grace.

For it is God who is at work in you, enabling you both to will and to work for his good pleasure. (Phil 2:13)

God, working within us and through Jesus Savior, has given us freedom to desire and choose the good.

Reflection

In the excerpts above, Catherine underscores that engaging our free will is essential in order to respond out of our given capacity for love, in order to cooperate with the work of love for which God destined us. We are called to take responsibility for initiatives necessary to grow in the spiritual journey of transformation. Through her metaphors, Catherine teaches us about the balance between receptivity to God's love, recognition of need for that love, and the call to take initiative and responsibility. On the one hand, God has created us for love and freely gives us this love as Creator and through Jesus as Savior; nonetheless, we must engage our freedom to respond and take initiatives to live out of that love. Yet even this freedom to take initiatives can be compromised by our human weakness and requires that we use our freedom to appeal to God. For instance, I want to take time to pray every day; I have experienced the blessings of prayer, yet I become lazy, or I persuade myself that a whole list of other tasks is more pressing. When I let go of my prayer time, my freedom to choose has been compromised by normal human weakness. So, I need to ask God for help to empower my freedom to choose what I really want—prayer time. This example shows us we have freedom that must be engaged, though at times we may need help from God to actualize that very freedom.

Our freedom, then, is not absolute; we must choose to engage our free will and at times ask for the grace to have the commitment and courage to engage this will. It is important to notice that in our vulnerability we can be deceived by attitudes and sentiments that are in themselves valuable. For instance, we might tell ourselves, "I rely totally on God," "I put everything in God's hands," even in circumstances when I am called to take responsibility for initiating efforts that entail effort and struggle to live out. The spiritual journey requires a balance between surrender to God, reliance on God, and taking responsibility for engaging our free will. This balance entails a close relationship to God; it calls for the practice of entering into the silence of our inner cell in order to discern, with the help of the Spirit, the balance between relying only on God and choosing to engage our freedom.

In Letter 133 free will is a gardener that attends to the correct planting of the tree of love; in Catherine's overlapping metaphors both the tree and the gardener represent the person. This means that planting the tree in the nurturing soil of knowledge of self (humility), as gardener of my own self, the tree, I am invited to choose practices that allow me to know myself. I choose to take time to notice the ways in which I need God or the ways in which I act as though I do not need God. I find ways to monitor how I am self-preoccupied and inordinately self-focused. This self-knowledge will give me the information I need to seek God's grace.

In Letter 113, the person is envisioned akin to a sponge that has a capacity to absorb liquid, but in order to absorb liquid it needs to be placed in that fluid. Since I am both the sponge and the actor who handles the sponge, I need to make the choice to immerse myself in God's love which is the liquid that fills and empowers my capacity for love. I must take *responsibility* for immersing myself in God's love. This means I actively choose to allow time and space in my life to become silent and connect to God, to dwell in the inner cell. For while made to love, as a sponge is made to absorb liquid, I will not absorb the empowering and redemptive love of God unless I place myself in the liquid, which is in the presence of God.

In Letter 374, our capacity to love is envisioned as a precious gift, enabled and protected by Jesus Savior; yet our freedom to choose is also required in order to protect this precious gift. Speaking to a knight who in battle wore chain mail armor, Catherine tells him that the capacity to love is as valuable as his very life, which he protects with chain mail. If he protects his life, he equally needs to protect his capacity to love. All of us have the choice to protect the precious gift of capacity to love; it is like the choice of the knight to keep his chain mail armor on tightly. If he is not careful and loosens the armor, he becomes vulnerable in battle. In the same way, if we loosen the armor, that is, if we slacken our connection to God, our capacity to love either stagnates or diminishes, or we fall into unloving behaviors. Closeness to God protects our capacity to love as chain mail protects the very life of a knight.

The above passages highlight a key teaching in Catherine: God has given us a potential to love; we will be most fulfilled when living out of that potential. But we must choose to nurture and protect that potential like a gardener tending a garden, like a knight careful to adjust his armor well, like a sponge that has to be placed in water in order to fulfill its purpose.

Exercises

Grace: God, fill me with the clear and certain realization that I can choose the good when empowered by you.

Centering exercise

Phrase for monastic lectio: For freedom Christ has set us free (from Galatians above).

Imagination prayer exercises:

- A central point of the following exercise is to get in touch with the fact that we are created to absorb God's love, as a sponge is made to absorb liquid; with this awareness we can connect to the desire within us for that love. For, absorbing God's love should happen naturally; it is not something we must first deserve, or something alien to us that requires great effort to take in.

Perhaps before embarking on this exercise, it would help to remember ways in which you have felt that God cared for you through an answer to prayer, or an experience of healing, or one of forgiveness, or an experience of comfort and love as a result of a prayer experience. This might help you notice a feeling of desire for a return of those experiences of being cared about by God.

After centering yourself, imagine that you are a sponge that has been left to dry out. Notice this sponge and see what it is like to feel dried out and ready to absorb liquid; the liquid is God's love. See what image or insight the Spirit gives you about absorbing the liquid of God's love. Do you imagine sitting in meditation outdoors and receiving God's love with the rays of the sun that you absorb as a sponge absorbs water? Do you imagine jumping into a pool of water, where the water is God's love, so you are surrounded by God's love which you absorb as the water surrounds you? Do you imagine sitting before the Blessed Sacrament being filled with the presence of God? Perhaps you imagine some other way of absorbing God's love. Take time to absorb God's love.

- At another prayer period, focus on the metaphor about the knight's armor, keeping in mind that this armor protects the knight's very life. Remember that this metaphor tells us that protecting our spiritual well-being is as foundational as protecting our physical well-being. Protecting our spiritual well-being means protecting our conscious connection to God. Focusing on the importance of this spiritual task, ask the Spirit to help you notice what is the armor that you require or how you are being lax, not tightening your armor. Pay attention to any movement within that provides an answer, perhaps an insight, or an image. Pay attention, as even a subtle inner movement could be the Spirit's answer.

10

Angelic Food

Letter 26—God's Desire: Food of Angels

You might ask, "What is this angelic food?" My response is that it is God's desire, a desire that dwells in the "*affetto* of the soul" [deepest motivation emerging from the core of self] *where God's love dwells* and draws our desire to him so that the two desires become one [God's desire for us and our desire for God]....This food fills and satisfies the soul so that nothing else is appetizing, nor can she desire anything other than that which allows this food to be preserved and increased.

Scripture

I am my beloved's and his desire is for me. Make haste, my beloved and be like a gazelle or a young stag upon the mountains of spices! (Song 7:10; 8:14)

The wedding songs in the Old Testament Song of Solomon are included in the Bible because the Christian community considered that these songs about love and desire express God's desire for closeness to human persons. The mystics, especially those of medieval times, drew heavily from these texts to convey their experience of closeness to God.

Reflection

The above excerpt is full of wonderful metaphors, especially "angelic food." To understand what Catherine means by this term, let's start with her meaning for "*affetto* of the soul." In this context, *affetto* refers to the motivation and desire that emerge from the core of a person (the soul); or in different words, the preferences that emerge from the depth of our hearts and minds. God as Spirit, always present to us, also dwells in our core; the Spirit is present in the depth of our consciousness even when we are not aware of this. Because of this indwelling, our deepest motivation can become united to the Spirit's movements in the depth of our being; "*affetto* of the soul" refers to these deepest motivations that emerge from our core. For instance, a vocation or other call from God emerging as a desire from our core self is an example of this convergence of God's desire and our desire.

Through the concept "*affetto* of the soul" as applied to the metaphor of angelic food, Catherine offers what is almost certainly a mystical insight, an experience of God from which she learned a deep truth about God's relationship to humans. God, she tells us, wants our desires to be similar to God's; God wishes to draw the core of our motivational energy toward God's. This makes perfect sense. If God loves us and created us in God's image, then God would want our desires to be congruent with God's. Think about a relationship with a spouse or other very close, loved person. We want them to value what we value, and in important matters, we want their desires, preferences, and choices to be similar to ours. So Catherine is saying that through God's presence to our consciousness or the Spirit's action on our consciousness (different words for the same idea), God desires to attract us toward God's perspective.

This profound insight on Catherine's part offers much food for thought. Most of us tend to think about God as having expectations of us. We have to learn what those expectations are, and it can be difficult to sort that out. We can have an inner attitude that we must make big efforts to discover God's hidden and difficult-to-discern expectations. Yet Catherine tells us that God wants to draw our desires toward God's desires, that is, God's perspective of love and truth. God wants us to feel, think, and desire in a way that is congruent with God's values. And God is present in our consciousness ready to draw us toward God's perspectives. We just have to tune in! This last assertion reminds us of Catherine's repeated wisdom: she constantly urges that we develop a set of practices and way of life that make possible the connection to the depth of our consciousness. God waits there to reveal God's desires and perspective of love and unite these to ours.

"Angelic food," God's desire to draw us to self, is "food" in that it is nourishment for our souls or nutrition for our desire. Think about this metaphor. God's presence to our core is nourishment for our deepest motivation. So if we want our motivation to be ordered—fed by the Spirit—we must seek to consciously receive and "eat" the "angelic food" of God's presence dwelling in our core, a presence ready to move our consciousness.

Exercises

See instructions and guidelines for the different types of exercises in the introduction.

Grace: God, let me recognize that you wish to make your desires my desires.

Centering exercise

Phrase for monastic lectio: "I am my beloved's and his desire is for me." Song of Solomon above. (Think of God or Jesus as the beloved.)

Imagination prayer exercises:

- The following exercise seeks to help you get in touch with Catherine's insight that God desires to meld your desires with those of God. Become centered and allow yourself to ponder, to place in your consciousness the reality that God wants you to desire what God desires for you; and God's desires for you are those which will bring most meaning and well-being to your life. So wouldn't you want to choose to let those desires surface? Imagine a still small voice, the Spirit speaking to you about God's desires for you. Set up such a scenario in your imagination of a still small voice prompting you from the depth of your inner self. Then pay attention to any insight or "aha" experience that allows you to enter into this experience. Finally, take time to dialogue with God about your experience.
- That God wants our desires to coincide with those of God offers wisdom about discernment. Allow yourself to hold this insight in your awareness. Then think about a decision or choice

you are trying to make and that you wish to be congruent with God's will. Allowing the above insight to resonate within you for a bit, ask yourself, what would God desire regarding the issue you are concerned with? Ask the Spirit to inspire you and listen carefully. You may want to dialogue with God about whatever surfaces. Or you may sense God's desires are very different from the choice you had in mind. God wants us to be free, so dialogue with God or even argue with God and see what emerges.

11

Angelic Food and Transformation

Letter 26—The Virtues and Angelic Food

While we are pilgrims in this life, this is a food [angelic food] that draws toward it the fragrance of the virtues, which are stewed on the fire of divine love and are eaten on the table of the cross. This means virtue is acquired with effort and hard work, rejecting one's selfish sensuality, and with force and violence cutting off the reign of self-centeredness from one's soul.

Scripture

Although he was a son, he learned obedience through what he suffered; and having been made perfect, he became the source of eternal salvation for all who obey him, having been designated by God a high priest according to the order of Melchizedek. (Heb 5:8–10)

While Jesus did not need transformation, as a human person he learned and grew through struggles. As sinful humans, our struggles, sorrows, and failures—lived with God—lead to both growth and transformation.

Reflection

In her metaphorical language Catherine tells us that consuming angelic food is transforming and that this journey of transformation passes through the cross. Before we unpack what Catherine tells us here, we first need to understand what Catherine means by virtue. In medieval times, transformation and growth were often described in terms of growth in virtues. Today we might speak of how compassionate and kind or how understanding someone is. In Catherine's day these types of characterizations occurred in terms of the virtues. In medieval times there was a variety of lists of virtues in use, though perhaps the most common was that of the "heavenly" virtues, namely, humility, patience, chastity, gratitude, diligence, temperance, and charity as the overarching virtue (charity here means love as we have been defining it, namely, the capacity to care for the good of the other). Indeed, Catherine often referred to charity as the mother of all virtues, for the other virtues are related to the capacity to care for the good of the other. We have already seen that humility has to do with recognizing how much we need God in order to actualize who we are meant to be, capable of love. Patience is part of love in terms of bearing with others with kindness, understanding, and compassion. It also involves the capacity to trust in God's providence, which enables us to order our lives more faithfully to God's will. Gratitude most often relates to the recognition of God's blessings (another term for knowledge of God) and the related practice of praising and thanking God, an expression of love for God. Catherine referred frequently to chastity, by which she meant being ordered in one's relationships depending on one's state in life, assuming that living a relationship in an ordered manner implied living it according to God's love. Catherine occasionally referred to diligence and almost never to temperance. Diligence is the virtue of engaging with others and in our life's work with focus and perseverance, attitudes that show care for the other and for our mission and vocation in life. Living according to the virtues means, then, living according to God's love.

Now we can return to exploring Catherine's profound insight about angelic food in this chapter's excerpt. We recall that by angelic food Catherine means that God wants our desire to be congruent with God's desire. God wants us to feel and think and choose as God would, always rooted in love; and because God dwells at the core of our being, God's very presence feeds our desire so that it can become more congruent with God's. When Catherine says in this passage that angelic food "draws toward it the fragrance of the virtues," she means that as we allow ourselves to be fed by God's desire through connection with God, our own desires are transformed. When our desires are transformed, then we act in ways congruent with God's will, which means that we act in ways that are virtuous.

Notice how the marvelous metaphor of angelic food shifts a common perspective we often have about God's will—at least emotionally. It is not a case of doing God's will "or else," but rather a case of allowing God's indwelling desires to entice us as a fragrance entices.

In this meditation Catherine underscores that evolution of our desire so that it becomes increasingly congruent with God's desire even when it involves cross experiences. The virtues "are eaten on the cross," Catherine tells us. This is her metaphorical, poetic language to say that virtues such as patience, strength (fortitude), humility, diligence, and certainly charity are often forged or increased as we pass through difficulties, trials, sufferings, and conflicts and allow these to be touched by Jesus's redemptive love—his giving of his life for us; for God's angelic food encompasses God's desire for our redemption. God, then, desires that all cross experiences become opportunities for growth in capacity for love—living virtuously. For instance, cross experiences lived united to God's grace can teach us the most valued quality of compassion (included in the virtue of charity) and can enable us to learn patience with others and ourselves; such experiences can lead to growth in strength (fortitude) and perseverance.

Through an overlapping metaphor, Catherine emphasizes the arduous nature of becoming transformed even as we are enticed by God's desire to transform our desire. Transformation of desire is like being stewed. What does this metaphor suggest? We visualize a cauldron filled with God's love, a "love-liquid" that slowly cooks our capacity to care for the good of the other. We can imagine the cooking process of several hours in a slow cooker. If you slowly stew beef and vegetables, the final product, the beef stew, is very different from the collection of raw products that went into the pot. And the change from raw products to beef stew happens through boiling, a rather powerful process. If our transformation into persons capable of living the virtues is similar to raw ingredients being boiled slowly into a stew, the implication is that the process of our "raw" self being transformed requires time and a powerful process, one that only the potency of God's transforming love can accomplish. Just as the raw ingredients would not be cooked if not immersed in liquid with the heat source turned on, we would not be transformed if we do not allow ourselves to be immersed in God's transforming love. God desires to "stew us" into transformed persons, but God does not force us; we are invited to choose to take time to become stewed.

Exercises

This reflection is particularly rich, so I suggest you do the exercises below in several sessions, perhaps interspersed with other exercises in this book. Should you need clarification about the exercises below, the introduction offers instructions and guidelines for the different types of exercises.

Grace: May I persevere, my God, through difficulties and challenges so that with your love these trials can lead to growth and transformation.

Centering exercise

Phrase for monastic lectio: I want to be stewed and converted in the fire of God's love.

Imagination prayer exercises:

- After becoming centered and asking the Spirit to guide your prayer, envisage a pot into which you place beef, vegetables, herbs, water, and wine, and then you stew all of this until it is transformed into a delicious beef stew. Let this image inspire you to desire the sort of transformation that came about for the beef and vegetables. The following exercise aims to help you place yourself in God's arms in order to be stewed by God's love, that is, changed and transformed. First, picture Jesus with his arms outstretched, or imagine the Spirit as a cloud, or God as a fire that warms but doesn't burn. Choose one of these. If Jesus, imagine allowing Jesus to hold you and lift you up to join him on the cross. If the Spirit, imagine that you lie down on a cloud, the Spirit, which envelops you. If God, imagine that you allow yourself to be warmed by the fire. In each case, you are choosing to let yourself be "put into" the embrace of God's love. What does God need to "cook" about who you are through this embrace? Spend time focusing on whatever emerges as an answer; trust that having asked for the grace of learning what God needs to "cook," God will act in the depth of your being. You may not feel anything; you may or may not have any new insights, but you can trust that, since with your free will you have chosen to ask God for transformation, God is acting within you. This can be a time to simply let go and trust that God is acting within you, or you may have insights surface about which you dialogue with God.

- Think about the virtues described in this reflection. In which of those characteristics do you need to grow? Then imagine embracing Jesus, or lying down on the cloud, or sitting by the fire, as metaphors for placing yourself in God's love, trusting that that love is making you more capable of living a particular virtue. This is a quiet meditation in which you focus on an image, and you allow God's presence to work within you.
- Ask God to help you recognize experiences of cross—suffering—that may have left you protective of yourself or resentful toward another or group of others. Would you like to invite God into these experiences? Place in your awareness Catherine's wisdom that God wants to unite God's love to your potential for love. God wants to bring healing to your wounds so that the

wounds can be transformed, enabling you to grow in some important human quality (virtue). Surrender to God for healing any wound that surfaces into consciousness. To do this prayer, you can use the images described above about connecting to one of the persons of the Trinity.

12

Memory, Understanding, and Will

Letter 241—Three Powers of the Soul

My dearest mother in Christ tender Jesus, I want you to follow this advice. I want you to love God's goodness within you and his boundless love, which you will find in the cell of self-knowledge. In this cell you will find God, who, as God, encompasses all that has being; and therefore, within yourself you will find memory, which holds and is made to hold the treasure of God's blessings. There you will find understanding, which makes possible our sharing in the wisdom of the Son of God, knowing and comprehending his will and realizing that he wants only our sanctification. Understanding all this, the soul [the person] cannot be disturbed or

> pained by anything that may come her way as she has learned that all is imbued with God's providence and his utmost love....I also want to tell you that in knowledge of yourself...you will find this *affetto* [drive toward love] in your soul, for the will is nothing more than love; *affetto* and all the will's drives are moved by nothing else but love. The will loves and hates that which the eye of understanding has seen and comprehended. And so, my dearest mother, it is true that you will find within the soul all of God, who gives tenderness, comfort, and consolation that cannot be disturbed by any situation, for the soul [the person] is made with capacity to carry out the will of God. This applies so long as the soul [the person] has discarded all selfish self-love, and all that is outside of God's will.

Scripture

> *The good person out of the good treasure of the heart produces good, and the evil person out of the evil treasure produces evil; for it is out of the abundance of the heart that the mouth speaks. (Luke 6:45)*

In the Gospels, the heart is the seat of our motivation and desire, the place of consciousness where the deepest aspirations and drives that shape our words and actions are rooted. This biblical understanding of "heart" is similar to Catherine's use of "soul."

Reflection

Early church fathers, including St. Augustine of Hippo, had the insight that if God is present in us, if we are created in the image of God, and if God is Trinity,[1] then the image of the Trinity should exist within us. Or put another way, human consciousness should in some way reflect the triune God, the God who is three persons in one. Following this logic, the church fathers came up with the constructs of memory, understanding, and will as three dimensions of human consciousness that reflect God's trinitarian reality. These are called the three powers of the soul. Catherine was not a theologian or philosopher, but she took up the language and tradition of the three powers of the soul in order to explain her insights about the dynamics of growth in transformation and closeness to God. In order to appreciate how to apply this aspect of Catherine's wisdom to our spiritual lives, let's look at what she means by memory, understanding, and will.

Memory involves bringing into consciousness our experience of God's gifts and graces, the ways we have felt God blessed us, healed us, gave us wisdom, and provided meaning for our life. For instance, when I sit in prayer worried about a present problem, I can renew hope remembering the ways God has guided me in the past. Or if I am struggling with conflict about a decision I must make, I remember how a process of discernment led to the grace of finding a peaceful solution. Or I feel gratitude for God's presence in my life, I decide to make sure to take time for prayer because I have learned that God blesses me with God's peace when I do.

Memory is also related to Catherine's belief that God dwells within us because we are created in the image of God. If God is part of our being, then some part of our consciousness must know this; accordingly, memory also involves awareness of this foundational reality about who we are. From this perspective, memory involves the intuition and faith that God is within us and responds to us. We *remember* we are part of God.

Understanding is a pivotal power of the soul. It is that dimension of our mind and consciousness capable of learning about God at a deep experiential level. With understanding we learn that God is love, that God loves us and wants our transformation. Spiritually, we acquire this knowledge-understanding through prayer, meditation, and meditative reflection; and cognitively we acquire this knowledge-understanding through information about God in the liturgy, in a homily, in a lecture or book. Through understanding we have the potential to perceive accurately when our intentions and actions are rooted in self-centeredness and therefore not rooted in God. Through understanding we discern what is rooted in God's love and what is disordered and sinful. Discernment, then, is a function of understanding.

The *will* is that part of consciousness that chooses and acts. It is driven and guided by *affetto*, the deepest motivations and desires emerging from our core (on *affetto* see also chapter 10). Motivation and desire are in turn molded in large part by understanding, that is, by what we learn and come to believe. When what we know and believe is ordered and true, our motivations and desires become converted toward God's love, God's truth and values. In other words, that which drives our choices will reflect what is ordered in God. So Catherine teaches that *affetto*—deepest desire, motivation—requires transformation so that our will is steered to choose and act according to God's view of reality, according to God's values and will.

Our will—the capacity to choose and act—is driven not only by *affetto* and the cognitive dimension of understanding, but also by memory—that is, by previously experienced faith and trust in God and recollection of all God has already done for me. Accordingly, awareness of God's blessings and spiritual and cognitive knowledge about God ideally come together to inform our choices, aiding us in distinguishing what is rooted in self-centeredness and recognizing that which is rooted in God's law of love. For instance, I remember how God has helped me in certain difficult situations. This helps me have confidence in God's assistance (knowledge of God);

at the same time, I recollect that I need grace to overcome my weaknesses in dealing with this situation (knowledge of self). Memory and knowledge of God and self thus come together to open my understanding to better discernment and management of a particular situation.

So, to recapitulate, a person living in openness to conversion and spiritual growth remembers God's blessings, seeks to know God and about God's truth, and opens her heart to knowing herself before God. In this way her deepest desires and motivation are transformed and made, through grace, increasingly congruent with God so that her choices and acts mirror this transformation.

How is Catherine's wisdom about memory, understanding, and will relevant to our spiritual lives? The concept of memory highlights that consciously remembering the ways in which God has been present to our lives nurtures the relationship with God. For instance, if every day we took a moment to bring into consciousness ways in which God has blessed us that day, we would deepen our gratitude and felt sense of God's reality in our lives. Or once a week we might take fifteen minutes of prayer time to remember significant ways in which God has intervened in our lives that week. Or we could take time to remember an experience of daily life when we felt God's presence as a result of a liturgy, a beautiful and awe-filled moment in nature, or a particularly tender and precious interaction with our child or spouse or a friend.

Catherine's wisdom about *affetto*, about the deep inherent drive that moves our longings and aspirations, helps us focus on examining our desires and motivations, for ultimately the way we make choices in life is profoundly colored by these. And often longings, aspirations, and motivations remain unexamined, yet they drive our acts and choices. Catherine's wisdom challenges us to bring these into awareness and then to God for healing and transformation in order to live a life that more closely follows God's will.

While Catherine lived at a time when our understanding of the unconscious dimension of human motivation was not understood, her wisdom applies to contemporary knowledge about the unconscious. Often our self-centered behavior is due to the wounds of our lives. I was not loved well as a child, so I have difficulty learning to love. I was wounded by those who should have loved me, so I have become fearful and protective of myself. I was treated with anger and threats, and so I can be manipulative or abusive toward others. And there are many more examples of the ways our unconscious impels our aspirations, longings, and motivations. In this sense, any work we do to learn about our unconscious and its influence on our current perception and behavior can become a spiritual practice as well. We can invite God to help us with a process of psychological self-knowledge. God's grace can give us strength to pursue the process; God's grace can illuminate us in learning about ourselves; God's love can heal the wounds we discover.

Catherine's articulation about *understanding* highlights the importance of spiritual and cognitive formation, of nurturing our knowledge so that our deepest affective drives are made congruent with the biblical and theological wisdom of our Christian tradition. This is particularly important in our internet-driven world, where anyone can post or publish information and make it sound authoritative and true. Thus, in today's world we are especially challenged to seek sources of wisdom that our Christian tradition endorses, to seek God-centered inputs to feed our knowledge. Consulting with wise members of our tradition becomes important in order to avoid following spiritual practices and beliefs that seem attractive but may not reflect the best of our Christian faith. We need to form ourselves through well selected spiritual reading, participation in liturgies, Bible study groups endorsed by our tradition; and we would do well to seek spiritual formation through reflection about our spiritual experience with a community or a spiritual director. Reflection and sharing about our spiritual knowledge-understanding enables insights to be corrected and deepened through the wisdom and authority of others mature in matters of faith.

In summary, memory, understanding, and will help us to think about different dimensions of consciousness significant for a spiritual journey of growth in capacity to love. Recognizing these different dimensions in ourselves and choosing activities to nurture each dimension gives an outline for a spiritual path. Memory means we should focus periodically on bringing to consciousness how God has acted in my life, how God has blessed me. Understanding highlights the importance of taking time to know about God and the spiritual life, to seek opportunities for formation. As well, understanding challenges us to be conscious of and reflect on our spiritual experience. And through the notion of *affetto* or our deepest desires and motivation moving our choices and actions, we are challenged to bring these to transformation through deeper knowledge of God and what is of God in dialogue with deeper knowledge of ourselves and how we need God.

Exercises

See instructions and guidelines for the different types of exercises in the introduction.

Grace: God, bring to my awareness the roots of my current motivations.

Centering exercise

Phrase for monastic lectio: I want to keep your blessings in mind.

Imagination prayer exercises:

- *Memory.* Take a period of prayer where you try to remember ways in which God has blessed you, where you have felt God's help and guidance either recently or in the past. Take time to offer prayers of gratitude; maybe you can find a psalm that expresses thanksgiving.
- *Affetto.* What do I most desire for my life or that of my family right now? What do I spend my time daydreaming about? Are these desires and dreams ones I would be proud to present to Jesus? What issues about my relationships at home or work occupy my mind wanderings? The answers to these questions often point to that which is most urgently motivating you at any given moment.

  Consider your motivation regarding your desires for those closest to you. For instance, I think my husband should change jobs. Where does this desire come from? Am I considering his well-being, what he would like or is good at? Or am I thinking about how much money he will make or how prestigious one or another form of employment would be?

  Bring your motivations to a dialogue with God.
- *Will.* Are you pondering a significant choice in your life right now? If so, examine what motivates you. Ask for the grace to recognize the different strands of desires and calculations that are moving your choice. Having noted these, ask the Spirit to help you see which are ordered, which perhaps not.

(See next chapter for exercises on *understanding*).

13

The Eye of Understanding

Letter 33—The Light of Faith

She is not shrouded in darkness, for her guide is the light of most holy faith, which is the pupil of the eye of understanding. Understanding guided by the light of faith steers *affetto* [deepest desire] toward that which should be loved, placing before *affetto* [will, capacity to choose] the love God has for her, and the teaching of Christ crucified. And so *affetto* [the will], seeing with the light that she is loved, is compelled to love and to show that she truly loves her Creator following the doctrine of truth [the way of God's love]....Through this path, and no other, we will acquire the life of grace.

Letter 51—Eye of the Soul

The true eye of our soul is understanding, which possesses the light of most holy faith; this is the case so long as the cloth of selfish self-love has not covered it up. When selfish self-love has been removed, the eye [of understanding] remains clear and can see....Then, experiencing that the eye of understanding is moved by *affetto,* it opens promptly and focuses on its object, Christ crucified, in whom—especially in his blood—he recognizes the abyss of Christ's immeasurable love.

Scripture

So also, no one comprehends what is truly God's except the Spirit of God. Now we have received not the spirit of the world, but the Spirit that is from God, so that we may understand the gifts bestowed on us by God. Those who are unspiritual do not receive the gifts of the Spirit, for they are foolishness to them, and they are unable to understand them because they are spiritually discerned. Those who are spiritual discern all things, and they are themselves subject to no one else's scrutiny. "For who has known the mind of the Lord so as to instruct him?" But we have the mind of Christ. (1 Cor 2:11–12, 14–16)

Paul teaches the Corinthians that those who are converted to belief in and adherence to Jesus of Nazareth and receive the Spirit become able to perceive correctly what comes from God.

Reflection

We said in the last chapter that understanding is a pivotal power of the soul, a pivotal dimension of consciousness for the spiritual journey of transformation. Accordingly, in this reflection we dig more deeply into other dimensions of Catherine's teaching about understanding through her metaphor of the "eye" of understanding, and the relationship of this "eye" to faith.

With the creativity of her mystical perception, Catherine visualized the understanding dimension of consciousness as an eye, the pupil of which is the light of faith. That understanding is an eye implies that this is the dimension of consciousness with which we see, with which we are able to distinguish and discern. Understanding is also the "eye of the soul," meaning that that which is seen and discerned through understanding about God and what is of God engages our deepest consciousness (our soul). For such seeing we require faith, which here means trust that God's love is operative in our lives, ready to manifest God's grace in our daily existence. This confidence and conviction about God's loving presence to us (faith) is like a light that illuminates and makes brightly visible to our consciousness God's love at work in our lives. Faith makes "seeing" more accurate as trust in God's love illuminates our perceptions in order to clearly see what must be chosen and rouses our longings so that we desire to act accordingly. We see what we should do and how we should act according to God's perspective.

Summarized in different words, if our eye of understanding is illuminated with the light of God's presence within us and we have trust in that light, we will interpret that which we experience, that which we learn, and all that occurs in our life in a balanced manner from the point of view of the Spirit. We will view our desires and possible actions in the light of concern for the good of the other rather than through the lens of self-centeredness.

Through the metaphor of the eye of understanding, Catherine underscores another aspect of her central theme about knowledge of God and self. When we learn experientially, with our deepest affective core, that God loves us, our human motivation, our impulse will be to love back; as Catherine tells us above, "Seeing that she [the person] is loved, she is compelled to love." Knowing ourselves loved by God is the deepest, most effective motivating force that stirs our desire to seek and find ways of loving God back. And loving God back involves engaging in life in a converted way, living according to God's values; this implies giving of ourselves according to our life reality and vocation.

However, our eye of understanding—our capacity to see and recognize—can be impaired. In Letter 51 Catherine highlights that self-centeredness is that cloth which prevents us from recognizing the implications for our lives of our central Christian belief, that Christ gave his life for us. Our tendency to prioritize ourselves in a disordered way makes it hard to emotionally pay attention to and accept a crucified savior whom we are meant to imitate in his willingness to give of himself no matter the cost to him. Our human vulnerability to avoid, to not "see," what is costly to us is countered with the light of faith, that is, trust in God. Without the light of faith—trust in God—we are less likely to take in and accept that letting go of self is required to care for the good of the other; we are less likely to accept that challenges, stressors, and difficulties are likely to be involved in following God's will. Thus, one of God's "perspectives" that understanding must grasp, that the eye must see, is that the path of love and following of God's will involves the cross. This reality is central to the Christian faith, for it was out of love and care for us that God limited self, becoming a human person in Jesus, who, though also God, lived his vocation to teach the truth, to heal and free us from sin, while enduring misinterpretation of his actions and motivations and enduring unjust opposition that became violent and eventually required the offering of his very life. As followers of Christ, giving of self according to our calling is that which we are invited to imitate. We note that Jesus did not seek suffering for the sake of suffering; rather faithfulness to what he was called to do brought misunderstanding and persecution and undoubtedly day to day difficulties that were part of being an itinerant preacher.

In short, in terms of Catherine's metaphor, the eye of understanding is clouded when we cannot accept that love and the cross—giving of self even when costly—are intertwined; that there is an inevitable relationship between care for the good of the other and willingness to let go of some of our priorities, and at times to endure discomfort, opposition, stress, and distress.

Exercises

See instructions and guidelines for the different types of exercises in the introduction.

Grace: My God, may your light shine to dispel that which obscures my perception of your truth.

Centering exercise

Phrase for monastic lectio: Infuse me with faith and trust in you so that I may see clearly.

Imagination prayer exercises:

- Bring into your awareness Catherine's wisdom about "understanding" as a power of the soul; remember that "understanding" refers to our capacity to perceive and receive God's communication and learn the truth about God. After becoming quiet and centered, ask yourself, do you trust that you are capable of perceiving God's guidance, that God is present within you ready to inspire you, guide you, and help you? Notice that your first thoughts may be theoretical and may not reflect the way you actually behave. Many of us would immediately answer yes to this question and yet in practice act as if this were not a reality. So, ask yourself, do I actually behave as though God is always there, desiring to interact with me when I tune in? Do I consult the Spirit dwelling within me about important choices and decisions? If you consult the Spirit, do you listen in silence and with an open mind? Ask yourself these questions and listen. What surfaces in your consciousness? What do you want to say to God about what you have intuited? Perhaps you want to pray to have more trust that God is ready to communicate with you. Perhaps you want to ask for help recognizing the voice of God in your inner experience. Or perhaps you'll become aware of some issue in your life about which you would want to consult the Spirit, some decision about which you want light and guidance, that is, more *understanding*.

- The following reflections are for a new prayer period. We can easily pursue popular beliefs that do not reflect a Christian interpretation of God's wisdom and will, and so we take time to ask God to help us notice whether we hold beliefs that do not fully represent God's wisdom. For instance, many of us believe that "everything happens for a reason." Though based on some traditions of Christian piety, this belief is not theologically sound, for it implies that tragedies and even evil or sinful events are *sent or purposefully allowed by God*. But God does not *cause* tragedies or evil, any more than God caused Jesus's death.[1] Instead, Christian faith invites us to interpret tragedy and evil with our eyes set on Jesus's resurrection—the ultimate triumph over evil. In terms of living our lives, faith in the resurrection tells us that new life can come from any experience of sorrow and tragedy. This new life could be new wisdom and maturity, greater faith, more patience and compassion, or new ways of living our life constructively. For instance, think about parents who have started important causes that have benefitted many after forgiving those responsible for a child's death.

Having asked God for discernment and wisdom about your beliefs, dialogue with God about any belief that surfaces. After the prayer period you may wish to look into the grounded Christian teaching on any belief about which you have questions.

- Catherine's teaching about the eye of understanding and faith suggests ways of praying into the foregoing wisdom about a resurrection perspective on tragedy and evil. Opening the eye of understanding implies asking for light to discern God's perspective on whatever happens in our lives. The Spirit can illuminate our understanding and with trust in God (faith) we can see events in our lives in the light of God's wisdom. Petitions for faith to shine upon our perspective would seek God's loving viewpoint and assistance with tragic life situations. Take time to notice any experience of injustice, loss, tragedy, suffering that you may want to bring to God so that God's love can transform the experience into new life. Take time in prayer to dialogue with God about the experience and to listen for God's perspective. For serious experiences of tragedy and evil, we will undoubtedly need to pray many times and perhaps over long periods of time. We can trust that in time God brings new life from tragedy and evil when we seek God's transforming grace.

14

The Blood of Christ

Letter 73—*Affetto* and Christ's Blood

Love leaves no room for sadness or confusion, and therefore I desire that your *affetto* [desire and motivation emerging from one's core] be grounded in the blood. The blood will make you drunk; it will burn and consume all your selfish self-love; in so doing the fire of his [Christ's] love will douse the fire of fear and selfish self-love. Why is there fire in the blood? Because the blood was offered out of a most passionate fire of love....For you know that the power of the blood of the immaculate Lamb is due to the divine essence. Know that if he [Jesus] had been only a man, without union with God, his blood would have had no power. However, because of the union God formed with man, God received the sacrifice of his blood. And so this glorious blood is a perfumed ointment that cancels the stench of our iniquity....And, therefore, I want to see you immersed and bathed in the blood of the Son of God.

Letter 213—Christ's Blood Consumes Self-centeredness

This love is evidenced in the blood, shed out of overabundance of love and is contained in the vessel of our soul. You must pay attention and seek to know this love and drown yourself in the blood and allow yourself to burn in its fire, so that your selfish self-will is consumed. One must not settle for just saying the right number of Our Fathers.

Letter 305—The Wine Keeper

The truth is this, that God created us so that we might participate in his being and that we might enjoy his eternal, ultimate goodness. Who has announced and manifested this truth? The blood of the humble, spotless Lamb, whose vicar you [Pope Gregory XI] are. You are the wine keeper who has the keys to the blood which restored us to grace. One could say persons are born anew every time they are freed from mortal sin and receive the blood in confession. In this way—as we receive the blessings, the fruit of the blood—we repeatedly learn that the truth is revealed in the blood.

Scripture

This is the one who came by water and blood, Jesus Christ, not with the water only but with the water and the blood. And the Spirit is the one that testifies, for the Spirit is truth. And this is the testimony: God gave us eternal life, and this life is his Son. (1 John 5:6, 11)

After Jesus on the cross was pierced with the lance, his blood poured out until water flowed, indicating that all of Jesus's blood had been poured out. In Jesus's time it was believed that life was contained in the blood; so shedding all of one's blood meant giving all of one's life. Since the earliest Christian tradition, the blood of Christ has been a symbol of God's life given for us through Christ.

Reflection

Catherine's metaphors frequently lead to similar insights. Because these metaphors are meant to touch the heart and convey mystical understanding, each metaphor can stir us in a different way to appreciation and absorption of the wisdom Catherine wishes to communicate. In this reflection and the following two, we will explore the blood—one of Catherine's most frequent metaphors—which discloses in new ways themes we have already covered.

Catherine's metaphor of the blood follows biblical tradition. In Old Testament times people believed that life was contained in the blood, so that animals and persons died once blood left the body. Accordingly, animal sacrifices were offerings of life. In John's Gospel we are told that water followed blood after the lance pierced Jesus's side; in other words, Jesus gave all his blood and, therefore, all his life. The life contained in Jesus's blood is not just that which kept Jesus alive as a human; for believers, it is the life of God. Catherine tells us this in Letter 73 above, "the power of the blood of the immaculate Lamb is due to the divine essence." The blood of Jesus, then, is also the salvific life of God that enables our living according to the purpose for which we were created.

Catherine further compares the blood of Christ, filled with God's essence, with a perfumed ointment. This is a very suggestive metaphor, enlisting the sense of smell. Sometimes metaphors can be startling, in this way shaking our inner imagination into a new way of viewing a spiritual reality and empowering us to seek that reality. Catherine challenges us to imagine Jesus's saving life, his blood, as an ointment that can be applied to our body, bringing us well-being; as well this ointment emits a perfume that we can imagine as a scent that fills our being. We must try this metaphor in a prayer exercise to appreciate its power.

The metaphor in the second passage very directly addresses how we are to receive and take in Jesus's blood. Our being is like a sacred vessel or container into which Jesus's blood is meant to be poured. We are created to be a receptacle for the transforming fluid that flowed from Jesus's side and that includes the essence of God. This metaphor challenges us to consciously put forth our sacred vessel, ourselves, to receive the precious liquid, the blood.

At the end of the passage, Catherine tells us not to settle for "the right number of Our Fathers." She is saying that just reciting prayers, just being faithful to a routine of set prayers, is not enough. Our spiritual practice must include "drowning" ourselves in the blood of Christ, another startling metaphor. Drowning ourselves in the blood of Christ suggests immersion of our consciousness in God's life-presence which is within us. How do I immerse myself? By regular periods of silence in which I connect to God within and by practices that allow me to direct my attention to the reality of God within me and God present in all the events and tasks of my daily life.

The blood, God's saving essence given us through Christ, is dispensed through the sacraments. Here the metaphor of blood helps us to reflect on the fact that, for those who are Catholic Christians, participation in the sacraments is a way of electing to receive God's empowering life (grace) intentionally and consciously. Envisioning the sacraments as rituals that mediate the reception of Jesus's saving lifeblood can renew our practice. Going to Mass would not be an obligation or a customary ritual, but it would be experienced as a precious moment to receive Jesus's life, God's saving essence. Similarly, the sacrament of reconciliation is a moment for repentance, but also a moment to imagine one's weaknesses and failings bathed in and made better through the perfumed ointment of the blood of Christ. Baptism would not be just a customary ritual but a major moment of inviting God's life-giving grace into the life of a child welcomed into the Christian community.

Catherine took so seriously the significance of the sacraments in mediating Jesus's saving life that she admonished the pope to use his authority to ensure that the sacraments were administered with consciousness of their importance in offering the saving life of Christ. For Catherine was concerned about the disordered lives of many clerics who did not properly "dispense" the life-giving sacraments.

Exercises

See instructions and guidelines for the different types of exercises in the introduction.

Grace: God, give me new insight about Christ's blood as your very life and teach me to grow spiritually through this renewed insight.

Centering exercise

Phrase for monastic lectio: I am a container for the blood of Christ, God's life.

Imagination prayer exercises:

- Imagine being anointed with a perfumed ointment containing Jesus's lifeblood. Tell yourself this ointment is so fine and powerful that it can soothe and soften your weaknesses and woundedness. Use your sense of smell, which can be very helpful for entering into a meditation. Imagine breathing in a scent that communicates God's very life to your body and consciousness. Take time to sense what this startling metaphor stirs within you. Dialogue with God about this.

- After doing a centering exercise, imagine that your whole being is a container. Imagine the type of container you want to be for the exercise: a chalice, a wine glass, a pottery vase, a glass bowl? Then imagine that you are at the foot of the cross and the blood from Jesus's side, *as living water*, pours into your vessel (you). Imagine that you are filled with the presence of Jesus's blood—living water, which is love. Pay attention to your inner experience. What surfaces in your consciousness? Take time to dialogue with God based on that which emerges.
- You can also do a more contemplative exercise based on the image of the vessel. You can watch your breathing as you contemplate Jesus's lifeblood pouring into your vessel. Pay attention to your inner experience and ask yourself, what aspect of your faith or your experience needs to be bathed today by Jesus's lifeblood? Be still and watch Jesus's lifeblood pouring into your vessel while you trust that God is working on the experience you have brought to God in your prayer.

15

Christ's Blood and Knowledge of Self

Letter 73—Submerged in Christ's Blood

[There is a] darkness of disordered inner trouble that many times afflicts the soul [the person] under the semblance and guise of a foolish sort of humility. This inner trouble arises when thoughts surface from the heart saying, "Nothing that you do is pleasing and acceptable to God; you are damned." And as such inner trouble progresses, he [the evil one] penetrates this experience coloring it with humility and says, "You see, due to your sins, you are not worthy of grace and blessings." Thus, the person often ends up withdrawing from taking communion and from engaging in spiritual exercises. This is the sort of deception and darkness caused by the evil one.

If you, or anyone else, is submerged in the blood of the immaculate Lamb, you would be protected from such deceptions; and even if such deceptions should come to you, they will not take hold. They will be driven away by the living faith and hope you have placed in the blood....And so, my dearest daughter, arise with the ardor of love and do not become confused, rather say to yourself, "What comparison can there be between my sinfulness and the abundance of the blood shed with such fiery love?"

Scripture

But now in Christ Jesus you who were far off have been brought near in the blood of Christ. (Eph 2:13)

Jesus's blood is God's redemptive love that transforms.

Reflection

In this passage from Letter 73, we find Catherine's wisdom expressed through the metaphor of the blood together with her wisdom about a type of spiritual experience that she almost certainly lived through. At times Catherine must have felt discouraged and down about her spiritual practice, feeling she was not pleasing to God; and in the imaginary of Italian medieval popular devotion, she would have easily felt this was due to serious sinfulness or the action of evil spirits—spiritual beings who work against God. She felt that without being immersed in the blood, that is, without conscious connection to God's redemptive love present within us, forces contrary to God and her own negativity could infiltrate her thoughts to make her feel even more negatively about herself, to the point of feeling unworthy of receiving God's grace and even unworthy of receiving communion. (In medieval times, communion was not given daily, and piety emphasized unworthiness to receive it.)

Catherine's experience has parallels for today. Any of us

can feel discouraged about ourselves, about our progress regarding any number of efforts we are making at improving who we are. Or we may have failed at an important undertaking, or we may feel that we are responsible for the loss of a job, or a friendship, or a relationship with a significant other. We might review over and over what we did wrong and feel deep pain and discomfort. We may feel unlovable. Or we may indeed have acted in unloving or less than honest ways that leave us with healthy remorse that may fester and become harsh self-blame. Sometimes these feelings carry over into our relationship with God. If I can't improve, if someone left me, if I made a serious mistake and feel a failure, I might feel that God must not be pleased with me, I might feel a sort of shame before God and even "avoid" God, as it were, by skipping times of silence and connection with my inner self. (Today most of us would not avoid communion over these experiences. We trust that through communion we receive Christ's blood—God's life essence to help us heal and grow.)

To deal with discouragement about ourselves and false self-negativity we can follow Catherine's advice to "submerge ourselves in the blood of the immaculate Lamb [Jesus]." We can take time to imagine partaking of Jesus's life-giving blood (see prayer exercises below and those for Pictorial Meditation 3). Such a meditation makes us receptive for the Spirit to penetrate our consciousness and bring order and perspective to our thoughts, restoring a more balanced and hopeful view of ourselves. We can receive the grace to recognize that we are imperfect but that is all right, because God loves us in our imperfection and helps us become better persons. We can see our faults or failures or a relationship breakdown in perspective and with inner peace. We become able to feel a healthy regret with hope of transformation and growth. We are able to accept truths about ourselves that can help us grow without feeling terrible about ourselves.

Catherine tells us here, as she does in all passages devoted to the central spiritual task of knowledge of self, that while wallowing in self-criticism and discouragement can be damaging, honest recognition of our failings is important for spiritual growth. Such self-awareness forms part of the knowledge of self that leads us to seek God out of our need. Thus, when Catherine speaks of experiencing that *we-are-not,* she refers to the recognition that we need God to actualize our potential; for God is being and love—"contained" in Jesus's blood. (In chapter 14 above, Catherine told us the blood contains God's essence.)

In short, meditations on the metaphor of the blood as God's life and love lead us to consciousness of God's acceptance of us as imperfect, as sinners, at the same time that God desires that we consciously receive God's refining love which empowers us to grow and improve.

Exercises

See instructions and guidelines for the different types of exercises in the introduction.

Grace: Protect me, my God, from deceiving myself.
Centering exercise
Phrase for monastic lectio: Submerged in Christ's life, I am protected from deceptions.
Imagination prayer exercises:

- After placing yourself in God's presence, allow yourself to remember times when you felt psychologically or spiritually troubled, discouraged about yourself, or sensed a painful inner shame. Now bring to your awareness Catherine's wisdom about being protected from self-deception through Jesus's blood. As you continue to be conscious of the ways in which you have been troubled or discouraged, visualize talking to Jesus about your feelings and imagine Jesus responding by offering you the bread and wine, his body and blood. Or perhaps you sense Jesus telling you that he has given his life for you and there is no need to feel bad about yourself or feel ashamed. Or you may simply experience an inspiration by the Spirit reassuring you that Jesus's love and life (his blood) are there to restore your strength and your positive view of yourself.

- If you got in touch with remorse, ask the Spirit to help you acknowledge to yourself and to God sorrow for wrong behavior in a way that is healing and not self-destructive. Remind yourself that Jesus's lifeblood mediates God's mercy and compassion. Ask for forgiveness and healing of self-negativity. Then take time in silence waiting for a shift inside yourself so that you are reassured about God's compassion and so that you notice that any unhealthy self-reproach diminishes.
- Consider Pictorial Meditation 3. Imagine taking some of the blood of Christ, visualized as life-giving water, and pour that water over yourself. As you do this, imagine that you are allowing yourself to be bathed and cleansed by Jesus's very life, leaving you with new freedom from regret or guilt and empowering you to do better another time.

16

Christ's Blood as Mortar

Letter 181—God, Master Stonemason

Our benevolent master stonemason [God] is so good! He knows so well what materials are needed to build what is necessary within us! Having seen that water did not work in order to mix the mortar needed to set the stones—that is, the real, benevolent virtues—he went further, giving us the blood of his only-begotten Son.

Letter 36—Christ's Blood Fortifies Building Blocks of Our Self

[Catherine prays:] "Oh boundless, tender love, you have united humans with their Creator and molded them to him; you have acted as one would when building with stones, fitting each stone to the other; and so that the wind cannot tumble them, he places living mortar [the blood] mixed with water. You, incarnate Word, through your union with human nature, have cemented the stone of humanity by attaching humanity to their Creator through your blood, mixing in the divine essence as living mortar. You have thus made provision for times of contrary winds that bring battles and temptation; for times of many sufferings and of torments that assail us to afflict our soul due to the evil one or to other persons or to one's own flesh. I recognize, first Truth, that due to the blood that holds us together, the wall is so strong that no contrary wind can topple it. And so, my most tender Love, we humans have abundant cause to love you alone and to have no fear of any deceptions that should assail us."

And so I ask you, my dear sons in Christ tender Jesus, never fear but trust in the blood of Christ crucified. Never fear; neither due to inner urges and dissolute fantasies, nor due to fear that you will not persevere, nor due to fear of the struggles that might arise as you keep obedience to your Order, nor due to anything else that might occur; never fear....So, I don't want you to ever fear again; may all servile fear be torn from you. Instead, say what dear Paul said; he who was so in love and who responded to the lukewarmness of his heart and the delusions of the evil one uttering, "Oh my soul, endure today! For Christ crucified I can do anything, for he is within me strengthening me through desire and love" [Phil 4:13].

Scripture

This cup that is poured out for you is the new covenant in my blood. (Luke 22:20)

The blood of Christ seals God's new offer of redemption—the new covenant—of salvation, of healing and transformation.

Reflection

In the above excerpts the blood mixed into the mortar is the very life of Christ; it is God's saving love. We keep this meaning in mind when reflecting on these passages.

Catherine imagines God as a master stonemason who wants to make a strong, secure stone wall of the sort used in medieval buildings and fortifications. To make the wall thoroughly sturdy, God mixes the blood of Christ with the mortar, thereby making the mortar extremely strong and protecting the stone structure from deteriorating or from partially or wholly collapsing. The wall is our consciousness and our personality, our way of being in life. God willed Christ's lifeblood to be mortar in the construction of who we are. That is, when Jesus's lifeblood is mixed into who we are and into the motivation-desire deep within us, we grow in virtue and our virtues, the stones, are solidly held together (on virtue, see chapter 11). This metaphor is another way of imagining that God offers the blood of Christ, God's life, to enable and protect our capacity for goodness. Catherine's metaphor of the blood mixed into the mortar is a reference to the foundational gospel teaching that Jesus has saved us through his death and resurrection. Through her creative metaphor Catherine invites us to enter into this mystery and avail ourselves of this grace.

Letter 36 offers a similar message. Catherine tells us that mixing Christ's blood with the mortar is a way of uniting us to God, building God's love into who we are. This metaphor underscores that God wishes to strengthen us with Christ's blood blended into the mortar that cements the stones of our identity and character. Building into our identity the life of Christ invests us with a strength that makes possible passing through sufferings emotionally and/or physically. It enables us to endure stress, injustice, and other forms of hardship in the course of pursuing our lifework. It strengthens us to endure spiritual distress because we cannot connect to God or when we feel that our efforts at prayer are failing. The mortar of Jesus's life built into who we are allows us to live through disappointment in our church community or the ministry of church leaders who have failed us. In short, knowing the weakness of God's beloved creatures, God builds into who we are the lifeblood of Christ. Accordingly, we are invited to open our consciousness and desire to this life-giving blood. And this blood, this life of God, when consciously received, gives us the strength and the meaning to go through life's trials.

The strength of having Jesus's lifeblood "mortared" into the structure of our being also invites us to surrender fear to God. There is fear of suffering, fear of commitment to difficult endeavors to which we might be called, fear of making mistakes, fear of what others will think about us; the list is long. Catherine herself recounts suffering from fear of failing God and fear of her weakness and sinfulness. Her mystical insight was that fear can be countered and dealt with through appeal to the blood (life) of Christ.

What do these reflections suggest for our life today? Imagining God as a master stonemason who has built into us Jesus's lifeblood invites us to a radical trust that God wants to assist us with life's emotional, spiritual, and moral challenges; we need not be afraid. God's strength is there within us, enabling our own strength [making us like a fortified wall]. We need to avail ourselves of this strength. We just have to have the discipline to "tune in."

Exercises

See instructions and guidelines for the different types of exercises in the introduction.

Grace: God, free me of fear with an outpouring of trust in your desire to offer me assistance and strength.

Centering exercise

Phrase for monastic lectio: You are my fortress and strength. I trust that your lifeblood dispels all fear.

Imagination prayer exercises:

- Imagine that God wants to build a fortress into which he invites you. The fortress is built with stones, and the mortar between the stones includes Christ's blood to make the fortress secure and safe. Pay attention to the love that motivates God's wish to offer you the gift of this fortress and the love involved in offering Jesus's lifeblood to strengthen the construction. Then imagine accepting the invitation to enter this fortress. Observe how safe you feel; allow yourself to trust in the safety of this space offered to you by God. Now bring into consciousness any current experience where you feel the need for strength. Imagine that this fortress allows the strength of Christ's lifeblood to flow into you. Perhaps it would help to imagine how sitting in a sauna steam penetrates one's body. In this same way Jesus's life infiltrates you while you sit in the fortress God has built for you, which includes the lifeblood of Jesus.
- An alternative or additional meditation involves visualizing God mixing Jesus's lifeblood into the

structure of your personality. How might you envision this? One option is to think about the Pixar movie from 2015, *Inside Out,* which depicts the main character's emotions as distinct personalities. Can you create an *Inside Out* movie in which you envision God giving a strengthening dose of Jesus's blood as communion to each aspect of your personality?

Pictorial Meditation 3

THE BLOOD OF CHRIST— LIFE-GIVING WATER

And so I ask you, my dear sons in Christ tender Jesus, never fear but trust in the blood of Christ crucified. (Letter 36) You must pay attention and seek to know this love and drown yourself in the blood and allow yourself to burn in its fire, so that your selfish self-will is consumed. One must not settle for just saying the right number of Our Fathers.

Letter 213

> The blood will make you drunk; it will burn and consume all your selfish self-love.... If you, or anyone else, is submerged in the blood of the immaculate Lamb, you would be protected from such deceptions; and even if such deceptions should come to you, they will not take hold. They will be driven away by the living faith and hope you have placed in the blood....I want to see you immersed and bathed in the blood of the Son of God.
>
> Letter 73

This image depicts the cross of Christ as fountain of blood—living water-Christ's saving life, that is poured out upon all, inviting us to partake of it. Catherine invites her correspondents to immerse themselves or to submerge themselves in the blood, Christ's saving life, even to drown themselves in the blood. We can contemplate this image and imagine jumping into the pool at the foot of the cross-fountain, allowing the living water, Christ's saving life, to cleanse us, to nourish us and to hold us afloat in the endeavor of life. Visualizing immersion in the blood invites contemplation of Jesus's life washing us clean of self-centeredness, a key task of the spiritual life. To drown in the blood suggests allowing Christ's life to totally fill us. So we can imagine jumping into the pool of living water and drinking our fill from it. Filled with the blood we become stronger, we shed our fear.

You may want to contemplate this image as you do the exercises in chapters 14, 15, and 16 about the blood.

17

Stairs Up the Body of Christ

Letter 120—Deepest Desire and Motivation Transformed

The first stair which he taught us to climb is that of the feet and *affetto* [deepest desire and motivation]. For as the feet carry the body, deepest desire and motivation (*affetto*) carry the soul. After climbing up to the feet, which are nailed and bound to the cross, your deepest motivation and desire, your capacity to love (*affetto*), will be stripped of disordered love. When you climb to the second stair, which is the open side of Christ crucified, you will encounter the secret of the heart; that is, you will learn with what immeasurable love he has bathed you in his blood. *Affetto* (deepest desire and motivation) comes up to the first stair and is stripped; on the second stair *affetto* tastes the love found in the open heart of Christ. Having seen the third stair and thus reaching the mouth of the Son of God, she is nourished with peace.

> For once the soul is clothed in the love of Christ crucified and stripped of warped selfish self-love that causes her inner conflict, she achieves patience so that every disappointment seems sweet. She can even rejoice in worldly persecutions and trials—from wherever God permits them—because she has found the peace of the mouth. [Such a person] tastes God with *affetto* of love and unites the mouth of holy desire to God's desire, and in God's desire she finds peace and tranquility.

Scripture

> *I have been crucified with Christ; and it is no longer I who live, but it is Christ who lives in me. And the life I now live in the flesh, I live by faith in the Son of God, who loved me and gave himself for me. (Gal 2:19–20)*

Paul shares his experience of being transformed. Who he is, what he thinks, desires, and chooses has become conformed to Christ.

Reflection

What are possible phases in the journey of transformation in capacity to love? Catherine does not focus on the theme of stages of growth or offer one template, as do some spiritual masters such as Teresa of Avila. Rather, in the letters and especially in *The Dialogue*, she offers two or three metaphors for stages of growth. The above extracts describe one version—there is another in *The Dialogue*—of her metaphor of the stairs up the body of Jesus, starting at Jesus's feet and going up to his mouth. Here Catherine describes conversion and spiritual growth in terms of stages in the transformation of *affetto*. *Affetto*, also covered in chapters 10 and 12, refers to the motivation and desire that arise out of our core, out of the place in our consciousness where we are connected to God. Thus, conversion and spiritual growth take place as our deepest motivation and desire are transformed so that these movements of our being become increasingly congruent with that which God values and desires for us. Our *affetto*-deepest desire-motivation is being forged anew as we grow in capacity to care for the good of our families, our friends, our coworkers or colleagues—and our well-being as well—and also to care for our town, our country, and the environment. This transformation of our motivation and desire from self-focus to other-focus is similar to that which Paul describes in the above scripture passage. He says, "*it is no longer I who live, but it is Christ who lives in me.*" Paul is trying to explain, also in metaphorical language, how he has been transformed as he has come to know Christ more and more, and as suffering and persecution have molded him increasingly into Jesus's apostle. Through conversion, Paul experiences that from the inside out, in a new and powerful way, he sees the world as Jesus would and acts much more like him. In her metaphor of the stairs of the body of Christ, Catherine describes three stages in this journey of transformation.

The first step in the transformation of *affetto* is at the feet of Christ, which are nailed and bound to the cross. The bound, nailed feet are a metaphor for the unfreedom in which we find ourselves when all our energies and attention are focused on ourselves in a self-centered way and when our consciousness, desires, and choices are distant from God. For Catherine imagines the state of unconsciousness about our vulnerabilities and need for God's grace as a state of being bound and rendered unfree; our *affetto* is not flowing freely toward love but is hampered by movement toward that which is disordered. Thus, the first step toward growth along the path of living out our capacity for love is to become self-aware regarding our wounds and sinful tendencies and about the disordered priorities and motivations of our lives. Often such awareness occurs as a result of changes within us brought about by suffering, struggles, disappointments, failures, and recognition of our errors, especially when these experiences are touched by God's mercy and healing. God's love gives us the grace to interpret these experiences in ways that empower transformation. We become able to let go, or as spiritual masters say, we grow in capacity to die to self. Paul himself tells us that experiences of the cross were important for his journey of transformation. When we gain awareness of that which is disordered or out of kilter in our life—Catherine would say, when we acquire self-knowledge—and seek closeness to God so that God's love might transform us, we are able to step up the ladder to the second step.

The second step up the body of Christ is the wound in his side. In her mystical experience, Catherine saw this wound as a path to the heart of Christ, where Christ's heart is a metaphor for God's immeasurable love and infinite compassion and desire for our good. This second stage is reached as with our *affetto*-desire we long to connect with God and we recognize in a deeply felt way the need for God. That is, this second stage is characterized both by the desire for connection to God and the clarity of recognition that we need God.

Note that this stage of knowledge about God's love has a cross dimension in that the heart is reached through a wound. This captures Catherine's own experience and insight that suffering borne with the conscious assistance of God results in profoundly felt knowledge of God's care for us. For we meet God's action in our lives when in our time of need we receive comfort, healing, and the grace to find meaning in suffering; these experiences cement our gratitude to God and the related increase in attachment to God. That the heart is reached through Jesus's wound also points to acceptance that faithfulness to God's call can entail struggles and distress encountered as part of accomplishing God's will. The person who has reached the second step is willing to follow Christ even when there are difficulties and sacrifices to be made along the way. Once we have learned enough about God's love and our *affetto*-desire-motivation has been transformed by this knowledge, our desire for God grows deeply and we are ready to go up to the third step.

The third step takes us to Christ's mouth, where we exchange a kiss of peace. In traditional contemplative language, the kiss is a metaphor for union, for the experience of deep closeness to God. For Catherine, this metaphor also implies that our *affetto*-desire-motivation has become so transformed that as, Paul says, Christ lives in us; that is, our desires and perceptions are so converted that they become as congruent as possible with God's desires, and this leads to peace.

We live in a deep, abiding peace when we are no longer at war with who we are meant to be, both as a unique person with a particular calling and as someone capable of care for the good of the other. When we have reached the mouth, we have developed humility and patience and can live, united to God's grace, with the inevitable and unchangeable disappointments, sorrows, and imperfections of life. This peace does not imply, however, lack of discernment to recognize when we are called to engage in possibly costly struggles for the betterment of our life or of some aspect of the life of our community.

Struggles and distress move over the surface of the deep peace of the mouth. For the peace that comes from being molded into persons whose lives are congruent with God's desires for us does not exclude the suffering that life may bring. Rather, we become capable of living through challenges, struggles, and suffering from a core place of rootedness in connection to God that gives an unfathomable, abiding peace despite the inevitable challenges of life.

Exercises

See instructions and guidelines for the different types of exercises in the introduction.

Grace: God, please transform my deepest desires and motivation.

Centering exercise

Phrase for monastic lectio: Christ who saved me, may my deepest desires reflect your presence within me.

Imagination prayer exercises:

- Consider Catherine's image of Christ's feet nailed to the cross as a metaphor for being bound and unfree because we are caught up in a self-centered view of our life. Ask Jesus or the Spirit to show you how this reality applies to you; ask that your consciousness be opened up to notice how you may be bound, stuck, or closed off by a view of your life that excludes the perspectives or requirements of others that should be part of your life. Be aware that God's love is always at hand to help you shift the self-centeredness of your view. All you need to do is become aware of that which needs change and with heartfelt desire want to have Jesus transform it. Ask for this grace. God's love will begin to act. The Spirit will show you how you can choose a different view of reality, and God will empower you to engage in different attitudes, choices, and behaviors. This is an exercise that works best when followed up over time.
- Contemplate the image of the wound at Christ's side. Can you visualize this wound as a path to the heart of Christ? Imagine moving into the

heart of Christ and resting there, if possible, without words. You might simply stay present to the image as a way of receiving God's love, a form of contemplative prayer. Or staying present to the image may stir something about your current life or it may summon a memory. Go with that which emerges; see what unfolds in your feelings, or what images surface, or what insights take hold as you remain present in meditation in the wound on the side of Christ. Dialogue with God about your experience.

18

Pray to Mother Mary

Letter 347

And since it is hard to protect ourselves, I want you always, first thing in the morning and every evening, to offer yourself to our tender mother Mary, asking her to be your advocate and defender for the love of that tender loving Word that she carried in her womb. Ask that she protect you from all trickery and alert you to any deception, so that the latter does not cause your defeat. I am sure that if you practice the sound principles I have described, she will accept your offer [of yourself] and will graciously receive your petition as Mother of grace and mercy for us sinners.

Scripture

When Jesus saw his mother and the disciple whom he loved standing beside her, he said to his mother, "Woman, here

> *is your son." Then he said to the disciple, "Here is your mother." (John 19:26–27)*

Just before his death, in bequeathing his mother to his disciple, Jesus gave us his mother to be our mother.

Reflection

As he is dying, Jesus entrusts a favorite disciple to his mother. The Christian community has interpreted this passage as referring not just to that disciple but to all of us who are Jesus's disciples. Mary represents the best human form of the love of parent for child. For God chose as mother to God's Son someone with a full capability to care for the good of the growing child Jesus. Catherine takes these beliefs to heart, trusting deeply in Mary's motherly care for her, often praying to her for assistance. She started all her letters by stating, "to Jesus Christ crucified and tender Mary," showing she called upon Mary in carrying out her ministry.

In the excerpt above, Catherine urges her correspondents—a group of knights who fought on behalf of Pope Urban VI—to seek Mary's intercession and develop a relationship with her to experience her motherly love and care. Even these warriors should entrust themselves to Mary and seek her protection, given the human vulnerability to deception and to being led astray.

Catherine believed that when we pause to develop a relationship with Mary, she becomes an intercessor before God and a heavenly person who can guide and aid us on the journey to growth in capacity to care for the good of the other. Catherine invites all of us to develop a relationship with Jesus's mother who can offer us tender motherly care and intercede for protection from all the pitfalls on the path to growth in capacity to love.

Exercises

See instructions and guidelines for the different types of exercises in the introduction.

Grace: May I experience God's motherly love through Mary, Jesus's mother.

Centering exercise

Phrase for monastic lectio: I hear Jesus address me directly, saying, "Here is your mother." I repeat this phrase as I imagine Jesus pointing to his mother, Mary.

Imagination prayer exercises:

- I invite readers who are not Catholic to consider the above scripture reading as Jesus's invitation to all of us to relate to his mother as someone in heaven intimate with God who can offer us motherly love in God's name. This involves approaching Mary as one might an angel, for instance, a heavenly being who can assist us. Mary is a unique heavenly being in that she is Jesus's mother.

  For those with a devotion to Mary, consider regularly asking for her intercession regarding your relationship with God, your capacity to discern and do God's will, your capacity to know yourself.
- In particular situations in which you feel a desire for help from Jesus's mother, imagine being with Mary, perhaps using whatever representation of Mary is most moving to you. Bring into your con-

sciousness that as Jesus's mother her capacity for motherly love and tenderness are perfect and she is there for you. Tell her about your concern or distress. Picture how she might offer you motherly comfort, and listen to her guidance.

Notes

Introduction

1. For a more extensive and documented discussion of these topics, see the introduction to Catherine of Siena, *Selected Letters of Catherine of Siena,* intro. and trans. Diana L. Villegas, Classics of Western Spirituality (Mahwah, NJ: Paulist Press, 2025).

2. For a well-informed and balanced contemporary biography of Catherine see Donald Brophy, *Catherine of Siena: A Passionate Life* (New York: Blue Bridge, 2010).

3. For those interested in Catherine's spirituality of political involvement, see Diana L. Villegas, "Catherine of Siena's Spirituality of Political Engagement," *HTS Teologiese Studies/Theological Studies* 77, no. 2 a6319 (2021): https://doi.org/10.4102/hts.v77i2.6319.

4. Most letters referred to in this work are found in Catherine of Siena, *Selected Letters of Catherine of Siena,* intro. and trans. Villegas.

5. Hagiography is a form of biography that tells a person's story in terms of their extraordinary spiritual experiences and extraordinary penances and sacrifices, sometimes the stuff of legend.

12. Memory, Understanding, and Will

1. Philosophers and theologians have offered many explanations about the Trinity. Here, to aid our spiritual journey, we keep in mind that the Trinity points to the fact that God is present in a personal way as Creator (not as an impersonal creative energy); God is fully present in the heart of each of us personally and individually as the Spirit who guides and empowers us; and God is fully present as human person in Jesus, our Savior.

13. The Eye of Understanding

1. This is a complicated topic that touches upon the question of why there is tragedy and evil if God is all loving and all powerful. Ultimately it is a question about how we understand God's love and compassion in the context of the existence of disorder and evil in creation. Much has been written on this topic and cannot be covered here.

For Further Reading

Catherine of Siena. *The Dialogue*. Introduced and translated by Suzanne Noffke. Classics of Western Spirituality. New York: Paulist Press, 1980.

———. *The Letters of Catherine of Siena*. Edited, introduced, and translated by Suzanne Noffke. 4 vols. Tempe: Arizona Center for Medieval and Renaissance Studies, 2000–2008.

———. *The Prayers of Catherine of Siena*. Translated by Suzanne Noffke. 2nd ed. San Jose, CA: Authors Choice Press, 2001.

———. *Selected Letters of Catherine of Siena*. Selected, translated, and introduced by Diana L. Villegas. Classics of Western Spirituality. Mahwah, NJ: Paulist Press, 2025.

Brophy, Donald. *Catherine of Siena: A Passionate Life*. New York: BlueBridge, 2010.

Hilkert, Mary Catherine. *Speaking with Authority: Catherine of Siena and the Voices of Women Today*. Mahwah, NJ: Paulist Press, 2008.

McDermott, Thomas. *Catherine of Siena: Spiritual Development in Her Life and Teaching*. Mahwah, NJ: Paulist Press, 2008.

Villegas, Diana L. "Catherine of Siena's Spirituality of Political Engagement." *HTS Teologiese Studies/Theological Studies* 77, no. 4, a6319 (2021). https://doi.org/10.4102/hts.v77i4.6319.

———. "Continuous Prayer in Catherine of Siena." *HTS Teologiese Studies/Theological Studies* 73, no. 3, a4611 (2017). https://doi.org/10.4102/hts.v73i3.4611.

———. "Examining Catherine of Siena's Controversial Discernments about Papal Politics." *HTS Teologiese Studies/Theological Studies* 77, no. 2, a6654 (2021). https://doi. org/10.4102/hts.v77i2.6654.

———. "The Spirituality of Catherine of Siena." 2022. Updated April, 2024. https://catherineofsiena-spirituality.org.

Clicking on https://doi.org in the foregoing articles gives free access.